EFFECTIVE SKILLS FOR CHILD-CARE WORKERS

Also from the Boys Town Press

EFFECTIVE SKILLS FOR CHILD-CARE WORKERS

Professional techniques that help deliver compassionate and quality care to youth

▶ **by Tom Dowd, M.A.**
J. Douglas Czyz
Susan E. O'Kane, M.S.
Amy Elofson, M.A.

BOYS TOWN Press

Boys Town, Nebraska

EFFECTIVE SKILLS
FOR CHILD-CARE WORKERS

Published by The Boys Town Press
Father Flanagan's Boys' Home
Boys Town, Nebraska 68010

ISBN-10: 0-938510-43-6
ISBN-13: 978-0-938510-43-7

Boys Town Press is the publishing division of Boys Town, a national organization serving children and families.

Publisher's Cataloging in Publication
(Prepared by Quality Books Inc.)

Effective Skills for child-care workers: a training
  manual from Boys Town / by Tom Dowd...
[et al.]. -- 1st ed.
   p. cm.
   Preassigned ISBN: 0-938510-43-6.
   Includes bibliographical references and index.

   1. Children--Institutional care--Handbooks,
manuals, etc. 2. Social skills in children--Study
and teaching--Handbooks, manuals, etc. 3. Child
care--Handbooks, manuals, etc. I. Dowd, Tom.

HV713.E34 1994   362.7'3
                                     QBI94-1501

15 14 13 11 10 9 8

Table of contents

Introduction

Since its founding in 1917 by Father Edward Flanagan, Boys Town has consistently pursued excellence in child care. The decades that have passed since then have brought two world wars, a great depression, a baby boom, increasing urbanization, social isolation, and rebellion. Social institutions have been assaulted and many have collapsed. Moral values have been put aside for social expediency. Throughout these years of turmoil, Boys Town has responded to the changing conditions in society and has continued to find answers to each new generation of problems. No matter how society has changed, Boys Town has remained true to its quest for excellence in child care.

Today, our children are challenged by increasingly complex and dangerous problems. The availability of drugs, youth runaways, aimlessness, sexual abuse, and suicide demand a response from our child-care organizations that is competent and humane. Our challenge today is to keep hope alive in the hearts of America's youth, many of whom face a seemingly hopeless world.

Father Flanagan's Boys' Home has responded to this challenge with the development of a model and philosophy of child care called the Boys Town Family Home Program. This model encompasses the essential components of family-style nurturing, behaviorally based instruction and training, and a "systems" approach to staff development and support in a home setting. On Boys Town's Home Campus, there are more than 80 such "Family Homes," each addressing the social, emotional, spiritual, and academic needs of a small group of boys or girls. In addition, mini-campuses have now been established in major cities around the country.

In 1979, the Boys Town Family Home Program was modified and incorporated into the Boys Town school system, and in 1988, the model was successfully adapted to other service settings, including Treatment Foster Family Services, Family Preservation Services, Common Sense Parenting, and Emergency Shelter Services. In 1989, further adaptations of the Boys Town Model resulted in its expansion into child and adolescent psychiatric settings.

For years, child-care agencies and direct-care staff members have asked, "What approach works best for kids?" Boys Town has studied this question and analyzed what and how staff members should be taught. The results of these studies and analyses are incorporated in this manual.

First, most child-care staff members need and want practical skills that apply to the situations they encounter. They don't want vague or theoretical answers that are not applicable in their setting. Rather, child-care staff members want very specific and concrete ways of acting that produce results. The purpose of the Boys Town Model and this manual is to identify practical methods or approaches to dealing with real situations.

Second, the Boys Town Model is skill-based. This manual teaches the practical skills staff members can incorporate into their daily interactions with kids. This does not mean that there isn't a theoretical basis for Boys Town's teaching approach; it simply means that theory needs to be applied practically. Theory, by itself, is not always helpful in addressing youth problem behaviors.

Third, most models of care have little research that demonstrates the effectiveness of their approach. Boys Town has been researching its approach since 1975. There are many published studies that illustrate the effectiveness of this approach.

Boys Town's approach to teaching troubled kids is behavioral in nature. Any system of behavior management must be implemented judiciously within a treatment program, and must be subject to ongoing evaluation and monitoring. Those programs that do not include systematic evaluation and quality assurance procedures appear most likely to rely on behavioral technologies that restrict, rather than increase, the amount of control a youth has over his or her own behavior (Kipnis, 1987). Although the staff development systems at Boys Town do not provide all the answers, they do challenge child-care workers to discover their true priorities in working with troubled young people and help them create a positive partnership with the youth in their care.

▶ Compassion and competence

Child-care workers not only care for youth; they care about youth. There are two kinds of caring: affective (compassionate) and effective (competent). Compassion (the heart) without competence (the head) is pure sentimentality. Competence without compassion is pure manipulation. Competent and compassionate child-care workers are good teachers because they have genuine feelings about the children in their care. Failing to show proper compassion amounts to ethical malpractice.

Compassionate child-care workers display many observable behaviors that help develop and strengthen relationships with young people.

Compassionate child-care workers:

- Listen
- Give compliments
- Joke (appropriately)
- Laugh at themselves
- Accept feedback appropriately
- Make positive statements
- Respect boundaries
- Use appropriate touching (pats on the back, hugs)
- Express care and concern often
- Smile and have fun with kids
- Resolve conflicts with kids appropriately
- Engage in events and activities that promote cohesion and self-esteem
- Give feedback appropriately

Compassion by itself, however, is not enough. Child-care workers who are not competent are not caregivers at all. A child-care worker who doesn't know what he or she is doing is going to hurt people or, at least, not help them get better. Failing to be adequately competent can lead to legal malpractice.

Competent child-care workers:

- Continually read and update themselves on information in their field
- Frequently give Effective Praise (Chapter 9)
- Provide counseling
- Model and teach social skills (Chapter 10)
- Use Intensive Teaching appropriately (Chapter 12)
- Teach kids self-government (Chapter 15)
- Teach kids to help other kids
- Teach kids to feel that they are unique, that they are connected to others, that they have power, and that they have models to live by

The whole issue of competence is the basis of Boys Town's skill-based training for child-care staff and administrators, our consultation process, and our need to evaluate. In order to work with troubled children and broken families, child-care workers must have both compassion and competence.

Boys Town's approach to working with troubled children has been successfully adapted by numerous child-care organizations. We believe that the mixture of compassion and competence that has been developed at Boys Town can benefit any organization that wants to improve the quality of care it provides for its children. We also hope that this manual can help you learn and grow as a child-care worker. The children are counting on you.

Treatment models and model comparisons

It is important when working with children to be aware of the different models of treatment that are available. You also should know how these various modalities would view the implementation of different forms of treatment.

At the end of each chapter, we will provide a comparison of six treatment models and explain how each would implement the treatment strategies or treatment aspect discussed in the chapter. The six models we will compare are the Psychodynamic Model (Medical Model), the Cognitive Model, the Behavioral Model, an Eclectic Model, Positive Peer Culture, and the Boys Town Model. (For purposes of comparison, an eclectic-based program developed by the University of Oklahoma will be used.) Technical and theoretical descriptions of each treatment approach and the sources of these descriptions are included at the end of this section.

Each of the six models has some very positive aspects and can be helpful in the treatment of troubled children. Children in crisis often have numerous problems and the use of more than one type of treatment often is what's best for the child.

For example, if a child has been sexually abused, he or she probably would benefit greatly from being in a residential treatment program that uses the Boys Town Model. This would help the child learn alternative behaviors to replace the ones the child has developed as a defense. At the same time, it also might be beneficial to have the child attend sessions with a therapist who uses the Psychodynamic (Medical) Model. This type of treatment could help the child come to grips with his or her abuse.

Remember that the main focus of any treatment should be helping and healing the child.

▶ The Psychodynamic Model (Medical Model)

Definition

Psychodynamic: 1. characterizing any psychological system that strives for explanation of behavior in terms of motives or drives; of a system that attributes causal efficiency to certain (or to all) psychological processes. 2. pertaining to psychoanalysis (This usage is unduly restrictive and unnecessary.) 3. of a psychological process that is changing, or is causing change.

Psychodynamics: the study of mind in action.

English, H.B., & English, A.C. (1958). **A comprehensive dictionary of psychological and psychoanalytical terms** (p. 418). New York: David McKay Company, Inc.

Psychodynamics: A system of psychoanalytic psychotherapy which emphasizes the need to counter the regressive trend in psychoanalytic treatment with a force toward progression. That is, a psychoanalytic treatment in which the patient, following a regressive trend, tends to parentify the therapist. In this system, the therapist counters this trend by not allowing himself to be pushed into the role of parent, thus bolstering the patient's self-confidence. There is an emphasis on understanding the patient in terms of motivation and control, the cultural context, and background and life-history.

Wolman, B.B. (1973). **Dictionary of behavioral science** (pp. 295- 296). New York: Van Nostrand Reinhold Company.

Description

A Psychodynamic Model (Medical Model) deals with the prevention, diagnosis, treatment, and care of mental illness and problems of personal adjustment.

Historically, this model grew up within the framework of medical care of the mentally ill. As the science and art developed, much of the model's treatment was not specifically medical, and many of those treated were not (in any ordinary sense of the word) ill, either somatically or mentally. The Psychodynamic Model is thus often indistinguishable from that of other specialties that deal with problems of psychological adjustment. The term "medical psychology" (more often used in Britain) is fairly descriptive of the practice of psychiatry but not of the curriculum of training in that field, which seldom includes any background in psychology of normal people.

The Psychodynamic Model (Medical Model) incorporates psychopharmacology, which is the study of chemical substances that affect the mind or mental states, and those substances' effects on behavior, emotions, and cognition.

English, H.B., & English, A.C. (1958). **A comprehensive dictionary of psychological and psychoanalytical terms** (p. 416). New York: David McKay Company, Inc.

The Cognitive Model

Definition

Cognitive Theory of Learning: A theory of learning which postulates the existence of intervening central processes in learning which are cognitive in nature, and which states that learning involves new ways of perceiving rather than of incorporating new responses into the behavior repertoire.

Wolman, B.B. (1973). **Dictionary of behavioral science** (p. 67). New York: Van Nostrand Reinhold Company.

Cognitive theory is an interpretation of the facts of learning that, more freely than other theories, postulates central brain processes as intermediary, that what is learned is a cognitive structure rather than a response, and (generally) that learning comes as a result of a restructuring of the individual's way of perceiving (insight).

English, H.B., & English, A.C. (1958). **A comprehensive dictionary of psychological and psychoanalytical terms** (p. 93). New York: David McKay Company, Inc.

Description

Our most comprehensive theory of cognitive development — that of Jean Piaget — portrays cognitive functioning as an aspect of biological functioning. Although Piaget did not deal much with deviant development, his theory deserves our extended attention here because it highlights so much that is central to human adaptive development.

According to Piaget, thought processes, like other adaptive processes, follow a maturational course rooted in the evolutionary history of the species. This means that cognition is at least partly structured according to a genetically transmitted plan. However, Piaget hypothesized that cognitive development is also shaped by three other factors. These are experience gained through interactions with the physical world; transmission of information by other people via language, modeling, and teaching; and a process Piaget called equilibration.

Three of the four contributors to development — maturation, experience, and social transmission of information — have counterparts in most theories. But the fourth contributor — equilibration — is unique to Piaget's theory. The central role of equilibration highlights aspects of development that most information-processing models fail to capture, even though Piaget agreed that thought processes form integrated systems resembling computers.

Piaget's (1977) concept of equilibration is based on his contention that cognitive development cannot be explained solely as a product of genetic programming and environmental contingencies. Instead, it involves progressive construction of new ways of knowing. One of the most striking characteristics of young children is their curiosity. This is evident when babies scrutinize their fingers, toes, and toys; when toddlers force their way into all kinds of forbidden but fascinating places; and when preschoolers incessantly question adults about the origin and meaning of things they encounter.

Although equilibration is hard to define, it signifies a crucial aspect of cognitive activity. The essence of this activity is a struggle to overcome gaps and contradictions in what is already known in order to gain more consistent, complete, and integrated knowledge. Because any problem can be conceptualized at many different levels, a cognitive equilibrium is often only temporary. Like scientists, children may be satisfied that they understand a phenomenon, but then find that new information requires new theories.

Why do humans struggle so for equilibration and then undermine their own solutions by seeking new information? We do not know. In fact, some children and many adults seem too readily satisfied with superficial solutions. Yet, most children (and at least some adults) derive great joy from cognitive mastery and will work hard for it. At the beach one day, for example, my three-year-old daughter crouched for a long time at the edge of the retreating waves, occasionally tossing a pebble with great care. At last, she jumped to her feet, clapped her hands over her head, and squealed with glee. When asked what she was doing, she replied, "I saw the water move some stones. And then I threw in stones to see if it always moves them. And it does! It always carries the stones away!" Here was a discovery that could delight a three-year-old, even though her conclusion would eventually be undermined and revised as she became aware of the multitude of variables involved.

To understand each level of cognitive functioning, we need to view it in relation to the overall course of development. Using Piaget as a guide, we can divide cognitive development into the four periods. These periods are marked by major transitions in children's thinking. The transitions are gradual, however, and reflect developmental processes that are continuous rather than jumping suddenly from one level to another. Because thought processes typically advance within each period as well as during the transitions, the systems of thought hypothesized to characterize each period are far from static. But each developmentally early system lacks certain qualities that the more advanced systems possess.

Achenbach, T.M. (1982). **Developmental psychopathology** (pp. 38-40). New York: John Wiley & Sons, Inc.

Piaget, J. (1977). **The development of thought equilibrium of cognitive structure**. New York: Viking Press.

▶ The Behavioral Model

Definition and description

Behaviorism is defined as a class of methods of changing unadaptive habits that is based on experimentally established paradigms. It is applicable to all unadaptive habits that have their origin in learning. The two major branches are classical conditioning, largely involving reciprocal inhibition and mainly applied to neuroses, and operant conditioning, applied to unadaptive motor habits, notably those habits of schizophrenics that have been acquired by learning.

B.F. Skinner sees behaviorism in the following manner: Behaviorism shapes behavior through manipulation of reinforcement to obtain the desired behavior. This theory claims that hypothetical emotional factors and mental states are useless data in the study of psychopathology. The overt behavior is the most important concept in this theory that is determined by external forces. Psychopathology is believed to result from underlearning or from learning inappropriate behaviors which are reshaped by externally given reinforcement.

Another behaviorist, John Wolpe, views behaviorism from this perspective: Behaviorism treats problems by using learning theory techniques. Problems are believed to originate when a drive-motivated behavior is arbitrarily punished, resulting in feelings of anxiety in similar situations. Therapy consists of reciprocal inhibition involving experimental extinction or counter-conditioning techniques. The patient is asked to perform the anxiety-arousing behavior in fantasy or fact in a rewarding atmosphere resulting in the elimination of inhibitions associated with the behavior.

Two major methods of behavior therapy are classical conditioning and instrumental conditioning. There are four forms of the latter method: reward training, avoidance learning, omission training, and punishment training.

Wolman, B.B. (1973). **Dictionary of behavioral science** (p. 42). New York: Van Nostrand Reinhold Company.

▶ Eclecticism

Definition and description

Eclecticism is a theoretical system with the selection and orderly combination of compatible features from diverse sources. It sometimes draws from otherwise incompatible theories and systems in an effort to find valid elements in all doctrines or theories to combine them into a harmonious whole. The resulting system is open to constant revision even in its major outlines.

A general temper of mind seems to determine the degree to which a systematizer seeks the maximum of rational order and overall consistency (with resulting temporary loss in inclusiveness and explanatory power), or the maximum of understanding of particular issues (with some loss in the tightness of organization). For the latter approach, eclecticism is an established term; for the former, no good name is current, but formalism perhaps describes its chief attribute. Formalism leads to the advocacy of competing schools and theories; eclecticism, though often called a school, is essentially the denial of schools.

Eclecticism is to be distinguished from unsystematic and uncritical combinations, for which the name is syncretism. Syncretism considers systems to be off base from their initial conception. The eclectic seeks as much consistency and order as is currently possible, but is unwilling to sacrifice conceptualizations that put meaning into a wide range of facts for the sake of what he is apt to think of as a premature and unworkable overall systematization. The formalist thus finds the eclectic's formulation too loose and uncritical. For his part, the eclectic finds formalism and schools too dogmatic and rigid, and too much inclined to reject, if not facts, at least helpful conceptualizations of fact. Few psychologists, however, occupy a fixed position on the continuum that runs from eclecticism and formalism.

English, H.B., & English, A.C. (1958). **A comprehensive dictionary of psychological and psychoanalytical terms** (p. 168). New York: David McKay Company, Inc.

▶ Positive Peer Culture

Definition and description

Positive Peer Culture (PPC) departs decisively from traditional approaches and charts a new course in the fields of education and treatment. A comprehensive strategy for dealing with the problems of youth, PPC teaches students to assume responsibility for helping one another.

Young people are profoundly influenced by associations with their peers. Too often, the peer group has been viewed only as a liability; too seldom has it been seen as a resource. Just as peer group influence can foster problems, so also can the peer process be used to solve problems.

Positive Peer Culture is not a new brand of group therapy that has just appeared on the market. Nor is PPC "something extra" that can be added to an existing program, as one might attach accessories to an automobile. Instead, PPC is a total system for building positive youth subcultures.

Although first developed for delinquent youth, PPC now is being employed in a wide range of settings. Schools, community programs, juvenile courts, group homes, and other child-care facilities have found PPC to be a clear and viable alternative to existing programs.

The history of PPC can be traced to Harry Vorrath's experiences at Highfields in the late 1950s. This residential treatment program for delinquent youth was established in a mansion given to the state of New Jersey by Charles A. Lindbergh. There, under the guidance of Lloyd McCorckle, Lovell Bixby, Albert Elias, and others, a peer-oriented treatment model called Guided Group Interaction was developed. In this approach structured peer groups met five times weekly in group counseling sessions, and youth assumed responsibility for one another's behavior outside the group meetings. The program at Highfields received wide attention as an innovative treatment design.

Following his experience at Highfields, Vorrath worked with colleagues to employ this model in a variety of community and institutional settings. In response to certain initial problems, the program was modified, expanded, and refined until it reached its present form. The result is a comprehensive and specific treatment methodology now known as Positive Peer Culture.

Built around groups of nine youth under the guidance of an adult leader, Positive Peer Culture is designed to "turn around" a negative youth subculture and mobilize the power of the peer group in a productive manner. Youth in PPC groups learn how to identify problems and how to work toward their resolution. In group sessions and in day-to-day activities the goal is to fully involve young people in the helping process.

In contrast to traditional treatment approaches, PPC does not ask whether a person wants to receive help but whether he is willing to give help. As the person gives and becomes of value to others he increases his own feelings of worthiness and builds a positive self-concept.

PPC does not avoid the challenge of troublesome youth; rebellious and strong-willed individuals, when redirected, have much to contribute. Those who have encountered many difficulties in their own lives are often in the best position to understand the problems of others.

Positive Peer Culture does not seek to impose specific rules but to teach basic values. If there is one rule, it would be that people must care for one another. Caring means wanting what is best for a person. Unfortunately, positive caring behavior is not always popular among youth. In fact, negative, harmful behavior frequently is more acceptable. Therefore, PPC uses specific procedures to foster caring behavior. Once caring becomes fashionable, hurting goes out of style.

Vorrath, H.H., & Brendtro, L.K. (1974). **Positive peer culture** (pp. 2-3). Chicago: Aldine Publishing Co.

▶ The Boys Town Model

Definition and description

The Boys Town Model has its basis in learning theory. While learning theory has adapted a mechanistic view of how a child learns, Boys Town's model combines a mechanism and organismic approach. Therefore, the Boys Town Model attempts to organize the Cognitive, Psychodynamic (Medical), Behavioral, and Positive Peer Culture models. Unlike the learning theorists, Boys Town sees the child in an active role in the learning process. External reinforcement is used until the behavior has been incorporated into the thinking and feelings of the child.

Model of development

The Boys Town Model was developed by learning theorists Elery Phillips, Montrose Wolf, and Dean Fixsen. In their approach, they combined reinforcement principles with the active involvement of the child. Unlike other learning theorists, they did not view children as passive or reactive to external forces or stimuli, like machines. Rather, the children are involved in their learning process. Reality is not grasped on the basis of copying theory of knowledge but rather by incorporating behaviors with their thinking and feelings.

Explanation of normal development

From the Boys Town point of view, behavior arises from the interaction of three primary casual sources: the biological effect on one's genetic makeup, the long-term environmental effects of one's social learning history, and the immediate effects of conditions that prevail in one's current social environment.

Explanation of abnormal/ atypical development

Abnormal or atypical development occurs as a result of genetics, social learning, and contingencies in the social environment. There is ample evidence to support the notion that hereditary factors can play a caused role in the development of behavior (Mattsson, Schalling, Olweus, Low, & Svensson, 1980). The long-term effects of a child's interactions with key people in their social environment also play an important role in contributing to the behavior of youth. Patterson's (1982) developmental model clearly illustrates how historical factors, such as poor parental discipline and monitoring early in the child's life, give rise to antisocial behavior and low self-esteem.

The role of early experience

While recognizing that behavior is learned and that reinforcement history is an important determination in behavioral development, the Boys Town Model attempts to focus on current conditions in light of genetic, social learning and present contingencies. The Boys Town Model states that while early experience is important, so too is the learning history of the current factors. The Boys Town Model assumes that behavior, as well as genetics and social learning history, are functions of environmental conditions. Early development is looked at as just another factor that needs to be considered.

The role of environment

While the Boys Town Model is proactive and active rather than passive and reactive, it emphasizes the critical role of environment. The environment consists of the range of stimuli that serve to elicit behavior, as in respondent behavior, or to reinforce behavior, as in operant conditioning. Inadequate reinforcement histories viewed in this context may thus result in a retarded or aberrant behavioral repertoire. This produces children with problems. Since children with problems were not involved in learning or were being taught inappropriately, they were not learning the social skills that are needed for positive development.

Basis of behavioral change

The Boys Town Model merges care, concern, and compassion with competency. The Boys Town Model uses teaching as a structure to build good relationships. New behaviors can be developed and strengthened through the use of behavioral techniques such as shaping and chaining. Behavioral change occurs as a result of reinforcing the appropriate use of social skills and giving negative consequences for inappropriate behavior. Change occurs behaviorally first, in an attempt to change thinking and feelings as the children become more comfortable and natural with their new skills.

Clinical implications

Given the assumption that all behaviors are learned, the acquisition of appropriate behaviors and inappropriate behaviors can be achieved through variations of learning, such as new learning, relearning, and unlearning. By changing behavior to be more appropriate, Boys Town is trying to teach the child to incorporate these new social skills in the hope that he or she will intersocialize the skill, which, in turn, can alter the child's thinking and feelings.

Mattsson, A., Schalling, D., Olweus, D., Low, H., & Svensson, J. (1980). Plasma testosterone, aggressive behavior, and personality dimensions in young male delinquents. **Journal of the American Academy of Child Psychiatry**, **19**, 476-490.

Patterson, G.R. (1982). **Coercive family process**. Eugene, OR: Castalia.

CHAPTER ONE

Professionalism

The Boys Town Family Home Program is a model of child-care treatment that has as one of its components the professionalization of child-care workers. Research indicates that while treatment provided in group or individual counseling or therapy is important, the child-care staff's role is crucial (Trieschman, Whittaker, Brendtro, & Wineman, 1979). In fact, the staff's role has enhanced the professional stature of the child-care field in general because it meets certain specified conditions that are considered necessary for a field or vocation to be deemed professional (Klein, 1975). These professional conditions include:

1. A professional vocation must possess a body of specialized and systemized knowledge and its techniques must result from tested experience.

2. The vocation or field must satisfy a broad social need.

3. Practitioners must give evidence of needed skills, skills that are both native and acquired.

The Boys Town Family Home Program fulfills these conditions. Initiated in 1973 as a method of child care, the technology is well specified and researched. The program, which is in operation in numerous child-care facilities around the country, provides child-care workers with extensive training.

▶ Child-care workers as professionals

Your responsibilities as a child-care worker require a commitment to work with troubled youth. Being professional means acting in ways that will benefit youth, the facility, other staff members, and the profession as a whole. Some of the "Do's" and "Don'ts" of professional behavior are listed here:

Do:

♦ Show enthusiasm for your organization and your position.

♦ Talk positively about your youth, focusing on their accomplishments, and what they're learning.

♦ Use good relationship skills like praise and empathy with youth.

♦ Advocate for your program and its methods.

♦ Be proud of your accomplishments.

♦ Advocate for the rights of youth in your behavior and that of your colleagues.

♦ Be prompt for all scheduled appointments.

♦ Maintain a professional appearance.

♦ Be an advocate for youth and their families.

♦ Share credit with your colleagues for program decisions and successes.

Don't:

♦ Complain about problems and the difficulties of your position.

♦ Tell "war stories" about your youth and dramatize their problems or shortcomings.

♦ Use an angry or threatening style, even in difficult situations.

♦ Criticize other treatment programs.

♦ Apologize or comment on inadequate performances.

♦ Permit any questionable child-care practice under any circumstances.

♦ Routinely arrive late for appointments or make excuses for tardiness.

♦ "Overdress" when working with youth or "underdress" when in public or during professional contacts.

♦ Blame or criticize youth or their families.

♦ Use "I" statements when presenting program decisions and successes.

Child care is a profession to the extent that child-care workers are granted the authority and status of a profession, and to the extent that they meet the recognized standards of their profession. Therefore, staff members must subscribe to a code of behavior if they are to succeed in their vocation. This code of behavior is represented by several major areas of behavior:

♦ Implementation of a well-specified set of skills

♦ Humane, effective child care

♦ Appropriate modeling

♦ Positive consumer relationships

♦ Communication and feedback

The remainder of this chapter explains these important aspects of the professionalism for child-care workers. Since giving and receiving feedback are two of the more essential skills for child-care workers, there is a major emphasis on those skills.

Implementation of Boys Town Family Home Program technology

At Boys Town and other facilities or programs that use our technology, daily emphasis on program implementation involves putting into practice the philosophy and skills of the Family Home Program to the benefit of each youth. This means that each day, staff members are teaching each youth what he or she needs to know to grow and develop physically, intellectually, and emotionally.

Humane, effective child care

Direct child care is hard work. A professional approach creates a humane, pleasant, and efficient working atmosphere. As a result, child-care workers have more time, energy, and ability to devote to helping youth. Not only does this approach help youth but it also results in a positive work environment that fosters success and happiness for the entire child-care staff.

Appropriate modeling

As professionals, child-care workers are role models for their youth and for their colleagues. By engaging in behaviors that are generally acceptable to society and to other professionals, they show their respect for others, improve their ability to work effec-tively on behalf of youth, and provide a good example for youth in their care. Additionally, child-care workers must "practice what they preach" and model the appropriate use of all curriculum skills. Youth can learn by imitating the child-care workers' appropriate use of humor, ability to express anger, sensitivity, morals, etc.

Positive consumer relationships

Positive relations with consumers are crucial to the success of a child-care facility. Consumers are those individuals and agencies who work cooperatively with the child-care facility for the benefit of each youth. Good relationships must exist between the child-care staff and consumer groups (e.g. parents, social service agencies, and school personnel) as well as with organizational members in general.

Communication and feedback

Clear, frequent, and pleasant communication is a hallmark of professionalism. With it, work can be done efficiently and smoothly. Without it, confusion and misunderstandings prohibit a productive work environment. Although organizations as a whole establish a groundwork for communication through policies and procedures, a number of other communication skills involve "being positive." A positive "can do" attitude is respected. Someone who cheerfully tackles new tasks, avoids complaining, and who readily and sincerely acknowledges the work and accomplishments of others, is a valued member of any professional community.

> **P**ositive communication skills
>
> 1. Giving compliments
>
> 2. Showing appreciation
>
> 3. Giving feedback pleasantly
>
> 4. Supporting criticism with solutions

The most important form of communication in any child-care facility is feedback. For professional growth to occur, staff members must value, solicit, and respond to feedback from others. Feedback is information about the effects of one's behavior on other people and the environment. Feedback can be positive or corrective in nature, and can come from anyone who sees or feels the results of another person's behavior. For example, a staff member could get positive or corrective feedback from a colleague for a simple behavior like turning on a light:

Positive social feedback — "Thanks for turning on the light."

Corrective social feedback — "Oh, that's too bright. Please turn the light off."

Feedback is essential to the child-care staff's day-to-day effectiveness in that it is a prerequisite for learning. It provides information about appropriate, productive behavior, and also provides information about behaviors or styles of interaction that need to be improved or changed. Thus, feedback informs people about behaviors they should continue, and about behaviors they should stop or modify.

Although feedback is imperative for personal and professional growth, it is not commonly or comfortably used in society. Every day, professionals, friends, family members, and coworkers participate in interactions that are pleasant or unpleasant, comfortable or uncomfortable, productive or counterproductive. Yet, people usually choose not to comment or provide feedback. Why? Because a lot of what people notice might involve personal behaviors, so they are difficult to talk about. Also, people who might not be accustomed to receiving feedback from others might be offended or react negatively, even when they are given positive feedback. In a child-care facility, these issues must be resolved very quickly. The child-care staff and youth must give and receive feedback every day to achieve treatment goals. The staff also must work cooperatively and comfortably with other professionals within the organization or in the youth's home community. This means appropriately giving and receiving feedback. The skills involved must become second nature to each staff member.

Giving feedback

Giving feedback is very important for building relationships, sharing information, and solving problems. Good relationships depend upon open communication and the mutual respect that grows out of caring enough to share sensitive information. Most problems do not just go away by ignoring them. Usually, feedback must be given to help find solutions to problems.

You will have numerous opportunities each day to give feedback to the youth in your care, to other organizational staff members, and to various consumers involved with the youth. Given the importance of feedback and the high frequency of its use, it is important to learn how to give feedback in a sensitive and constructive manner. The following list describes the nine steps of giving feedback. Using these steps will ensure that information is presented in a tactful, pleasant, and concerned manner, and will facilitate the person's understanding and acceptance of the information.

Steps in giving feedback

1. Be attentive — orient your body toward the person, smile, look at the person.

2. Request permission — ask the person if it is a good time to talk about something important.

3. Initiate the interaction pleasantly — start out with praise, empathy, or pleasant comments.

4. Specifically describe the situation — give the feedback in behaviorally specific terms without being judgmental, personal, or emotional.

5. Give rationales — unless the reasons are obvious, tell the person why the situation or behavior is important enough to merit your feedback.

6. Discuss the situation — be open to ideas or suggestions from the person; offer constructive alternatives or compromises as needed.

7. Thank the person for listening — let the person know that you appreciate the time spent to hear and consider the feedback.

8. Written feedback — if the feedback is complex or lengthy, it often helps to accompany the verbal discussion with written information that the person can take and review in more detail.

9. Follow-up — check back to see if the feedback had the desired effect and provide further feedback as needed.

Receiving feedback

Receiving feedback also requires a special set of skills. Given the importance of feedback and the difficulties many people experience in giving it, it is important for child-care staff members to encourage and solicit feedback. They come to realize that the only feedback that really hurts them is the feedback they do not receive. Most people may think they accept feedback well, but they do not understand that arguing or defending themselves, or offering long explanations actually punishes the person who is giving feedback to them. If staff members are not regularly receiving feedback from a variety of people, they need to check whether they are somehow punishing people for giving them feedback. This can be done by frequently asking for feedback (e.g. "Is there anything else I could be doing?" or "How do you think I handled that situation?"). Also, when someone cares enough to give positive or negative feedback, they need to be sincerely thanked for taking the time to share the information. A professional is careful not to do anything to discourage the flow of information and feedback. Accepting feedback gracefully and nonpersonally is not always easy but it is crucial to professional growth of each staff member and the success of the program. Here are the 10 steps of receiving feedback.

Steps in receiving feedback

1. Be attentive — look at the person, listen carefully, nod your head and give verbal acknowledgments, take notes.

2. Ask questions for clarification — ask a few questions, if necessary, to clarify what the feedback is about, but do not interrogate or appear to challenge the person.

3. Show concern — acknowledge the person's willingness to share information with you and show your concern.

4. Apologize (if appropriate) — apologize for any role you might have had in the problem.

5. Avoid excuses or interruptions — don't interrupt the person or try to explain your side of the situation at this point; just listen and try to reinforce the person for caring enough about you to share this information.

6. Discuss the situation — if the feedback is complex and requires discussion about how to solve a problem, ask for suggestions and focus on achieving a constructive solution.

7. Ask for more feedback — ask the person if there is anything else you can do.

8. Reinforce the person for the feedback — throughout the interaction and at the end, thank the person for being concerned and for sharing the information with you.

9. Request future feedback — ask the person to let you know if the situation occurs again.

10. Request follow-up — ask the person if you can check back in a few days or weeks to see whether the problem has been solved.

▶ Summary

Professionalism is a key element in providing quality child care to youth in treatment settings. To be accorded the status of a professional, child-care workers must possess program skills and make a commitment to work with troubled youth. A professional approach to caring for youth creates a pleasant and efficient working environment, and helps ensure that child-care workers are capable of meeting their responsibilities.

A major element of professionalism is the ability to give and receive feedback. Feedback is essential to a child-care staff's day-to-day existence because it provides information about appropriate, productive behavior, and behavior or interaction styles that need to be improved or changed. Feedback is shared not only among staff members, their supervisors, and the youth, but also among child-care workers and various consumers involved with the youth.

▶ Model comparisons

The comparison of the six models in this chapter will focus on identifying the professional in each program.

It is typical in the Psychodynamic (Medical) Model for a therapist or clinician to help a child trace his or her developmental lines through analysis and recollection.

Treatment is focused on fostering a change in the child's feelings about past events, which will then change the way he or she feels, and thus behaves, in the future. For this reason, the therapist, or counselor, is considered the professional in this situation since he or she is primarily responsible for guiding the therapy or treatment of the child.

The child-care staff members in this program are responsible for meeting the child's daily needs, but are not directly involved in the child's treatment. Due to the nature of their responsibilities, staff members typically are not considered the professionals in this mode of treatment. Consequently, the people who spend the most time with the child and who typically can have the greatest influence on the youth are usually the least skilled or trained.

As in the Psychodynamic Model, therapists are considered the professionals in the Cognitive Model. They would be viewed as the primary treatment agents as they provide opportunities for the child to act upon, structure, or restructure reality. Again, the child-care provider plays a necessary, but secondary role, with little or no input in the child's treatment plan.

In the Behavioral Model, the professional typically is the behaviorist who is doing clinical treatment with the child. The behaviorist analyzes the stimuli (consequent and antecedents) that are influencing the child's current behavior and then manipulates the environment to create a behavior change. The child is passively involved, simply responding to these changes while typically being unaware of the treatment. The child-care

staff may or may not be actively involved in the child's treatment.

In the Boys Town Model, the professionals are the child-care providers. They are the primary treatment providers and work actively with the child, using learning theory to teach the child new responses to situations. They also set up opportunities for the child to practice socially appropriate behavior with the goal of changing the child's thoughts and feelings over time.

The eclectic model developed by the University of Oklahoma also incorporates the child-care workers as the primary treatment agents for the child. Thus, they also would be considered the professionals in this model. The child-care worker can select a variety of strategies from several different treatment theories to implement with the child.

In a program using Positive Peer Culture, the child's peers are considered the professionals. The peers are primarily responsible for treatment, using opportunities to counsel and guide the child by confronting his or her thoughts and feelings. Typically, adults are involved in a secondary role, providing the program's structure and setting the ranges for treatment by peers.

CHAPTER TWO

Teaching social skills

As human beings, we live in social groups. We learn early in life that there are consequences, both positive and negative, attached to how we interact with others and how we choose to respond in social situations. This process of "socialization," which begins in the earliest interactions between infant and parent, prepares us for more complex situations later in childhood and adolescence. Ideally, lessons learned at each stage in a child's development become the tools that are used to successfully meet the demands of subsequent stages of life.

Today, however, our young people are challenged by an increasingly difficult world. Family problems, substance abuse, economic pressures, and the lure of gangs and delinquency threaten our children physically, emotionally, and spiritually. The tools required to successfully cope with these internal and external pressures include the ability to interact with others in socially acceptable ways and make appropriate decisions in social situations. The focus of this chapter is on the development of those abilities in children and adolescents, particularly those already at risk as a result of abuse or neglect, emotional or behavioral problems, or difficulties in learning. The curriculum of social skills presented in this chapter, as well as the techniques described for teaching these skills individually and in groups, have been used successfully for nearly 20 years as part of the Boys Town Family Home Program.

▶ The Boys Town Family Home Program

The Boys Town Family Home Program is a philosophy and a method of child care and treatment. The program is based on the belief that the youth it serves have not yet learned the skills necessary to live happy, productive lives. These youth also may be engaging in inappropriate behaviors to get their needs fulfilled because they lack a better behavioral repertoire. This treatment approach focuses on teaching these youth essential life skills necessary for successful transition into young adulthood in a "family style" treatment setting (Peter, 1986). Social, academic, and vocational skills, as well as spiritual values, are actively taught through reinforcement, practice and rehearsal, and a positive style of correction. The social skills contained in this chapter are an integral part of this system. The youth are taught behaviors that are believed to benefit them most and produce the best long-term rewards. The curriculum of skills and the techniques that are covered here form the cornerstone of treatment planning and active intervention at Boys Town, and can be integrated into a variety of residential and educational environments.

This chapter will focus on the development of social skills in children, the elements of social behavior, individual and group teaching techniques, planning skill-based treatment interventions for difficult youth problems, and the format of the Boys Town Social Skills Curriculum. The emphasis will be on viewing social skills instruction as a pervasive intervention strategy that can be used to address a variety of serious youth issues, including aggressive acting out, depression and suicidal behavior, delinquency, and school-related problems. The Social Skills Curriculum defines the positive alternative to many of the maladaptive and self-defeating behavior patterns in which a young person

may engage. It is intended to be an effective resource and tool for anyone working with children and adolescents.

▶ An overview of social skills instruction

The complexities of human social behavior become readily apparent upon examination of techniques for teaching a youth to be more socially skilled. Activities that many people find quite easy (carrying on a conversation, introducing oneself to a guest, etc.) can present major hurdles for a young person who has not developed a repertoire of effective social behaviors and whose deficiencies are compounded by emotional or behavioral issues. In addition, a youth who is capable of demonstrating appropriate social skills still may have difficulty in recognizing when, where, and with who to use a particular skill.

A youth also needs to learn how to read other people's social behaviors and cues. Successful social interactions depend, to a large part, on the ability to perceive and correctly interpret the nonverbal behaviors of others and to demonstrate sensitivity to their points of view and feelings (Hazel, Schumaker, Sherman, & Sheldon-Wildgen, 1983). All of these elements represent a complex social skill structure and level of integration that many youth will not develop without active intervention and teaching from the adults in their lives. This section focuses on the concept of social skills, the results of social skill deficiencies, and the importance of teaching social skills to children and youth with special needs.

The concept of social skills

Social skills, as a concept, can be elusive and difficult to define. In formulating a definition, as well as an approach to teaching social skills, we should consider how the value of each given skill is assessed, and by whom (Combs & Slaby, 1977). The value and meaning of a particular skill actually may be assessed from a number of different perspectives including: 1) the effect on the overall functioning of a group from an adult point of view (e.g. the teacher's assessment of appropriate skills for the classroom); 2) the effect on the youth's social standing from the point of view of his or her peers; or 3) the effect on the youth's own feelings of social competence and belonging.

Many adults who work with children and adolescents neglect to consider the potential discrepancies between these differing points of view. For example, a child's resistance to peer pressure may be considered very important by the adults responsible for his or her care, but may be negatively valued by the child's peer group and result in exclusion and a lowered sense of belonging. In fact, the awareness of peer group values and norms has been found to consistently correlate with peer group acceptance and popularity (Oden, 1980). Therefore, how we define, select, and teach social skills should be considered from the child's perspective, as well as that of the child's caregivers.

One frequently cited definition of social skills that attempts to take into account these differing perspectives refers to a social skill as the ability to interact with others in a given social context in specific ways that are socially acceptable or valued and, at the same time, personally beneficial, mutually beneficial, or beneficial primarily to others (Combs & Slaby, 1977). In this sense, social skills are sets of behaviors that do not necessarily remain constant, but may vary with the social context and particular situational demands. These skills also are seen as producing positive consequences for the individual (personally beneficial), but within the norms of societal acceptability and responsiveness to others.

The use of appropriate social skills also represents an immensely complex chain of rapidly occurring interpersonal events. The ability to perform a given skill actually is comprised of several crucial activities occurring nearly simultaneously. The socially competent person must: 1) initially be motivated to perform socially appropriate behaviors; 2) be able to perceive social situations accurately and identify which skill to use; 3) be able to decode and correctly interpret information from others; 4) perform the correct verbal and nonverbal responses that make up the skill; 5) be sensitive to social feedback; and 6) be able to integrate that feedback appropriately to enhance social interaction (Hazel et al., 1983). The enormity of this task for a youth with emotional or cognitive limitations is readily apparent. Many youth may have considerable difficulty in organizing and meshing their behaviors into smoothly flowing interactions with others, particularly under stressful conditions.

Skill performance steps

A socially competent child:

– discriminates situations

– picks up social cues

– uses appropriate verbal & nonverbal behavior

– receives and integrates social feedback

– adjusts behavior

– displays competent skill behavior

The task of staff members who are responsible for teaching the youth appropriate social behavior therefore becomes equally complex. This is due, in part, to the fact that learning a new skill is a skill in and of itself. For youth to benefit from social skills instruction, they need to be initially motivated to learn alternative ways of behaving, even if their motivation is external, and they need to be able to keep resistance and noncompliance to a minimum. In addition, each youth should have the verbal and motor capacity to perform the skill. On the other hand, you, as a child-care worker, must be willing to adjust your techniques, vocabulary, and own interpersonal behaviors to mesh with the learning style of each youth. Finally, the need for social skills instruction to present meaningful alternatives to a youth cannot be overemphasized. Social skills must have value to a youth, without sacrificing all peer group norms, in order to be learned and utilized in diverse situations.

In the Boys Town program, problem behaviors demonstrated by a youth are viewed as deficits in the youth's repertoire of skills and active, direct instruction is a key to remediation and growth. Positive, prosocial behaviors can be modeled, taught, and rewarded, and therefore, can become viable alternatives for the youth when he or she is confronted with situations that previously resulted in the youth getting in trouble. It has been theorized that adolescents who commit illegal acts do so because they do not have the skills necessary to achieve desired goals through legitimate means, not because of any intrinsic value present in breaking the law (Hazel et al., 1983). For these youth in particular, social skills instruction may present alternative paths for reaching an acceptable outcome, as well as a viable means of avoiding costly negative consequences.

▶ Correlates of social skill deficiencies

In some youth, deficits in social skill functioning are overt and unmistakable. These youth may be uncomfortable around people, lack appropriate humor, communicate poorly, etc. But the difficulties encountered by children and adolescents with ineffective social behavior and judgment go far beyond simply feeling uncomfortable in a conversation. The following problem areas have been associated with deficits in social skill functioning:

1. Aggressive and antisocial behavior: Numerous types of problems in social interaction style have been associated with verbally and physically aggressive behavior in children (including unpopularity), which has been shown to be a risk factor for delinquency and conduct problems (Kazdin, 1985; Goldstein, Sprafkin, Gershaw, & Klein, 1980). Social skills instruction has been used to decrease aggressive acting out in adolescent psychiatric patients (Elder, Edelstein, & Narick, 1979) and chronic antisocial behavior in inner-city students (Jones & Offord, 1989). The use of interpersonal aggression to coerce the behavior of others appears to frequently develop in families that experience external stressors, such as economic disadvantage, combined with a lack of appropriate problem-solving and child-management skills (Patterson, 1982).

2. Juvenile delinquency: The majority of social skills training programs and research has been directed toward juvenile delinquency in adolescents (LeCroy, 1983). Numerous studies have demonstrated a strong link between delinquent behavior and poor social interaction skills (Howing, Wodarski, Kurtz, & Gaudin, 1990; Long & Sherer, 1984; Kazdin, 1985). Institutionalized juvenile delinquents also have been shown to be particularly deficient in social skills knowledge (the ability to hypothetically pick the appropriate course of action in a problem situation), with those scoring lowest having the most severe behavioral problems (Veneziano & Veneziano, 1988).

3. Child abuse and neglect: Strong evidence exists to link the abuse and mistreatment of children, particularly early in life, to later deficits in social functioning (Howing et al., 1990). Abused children have been found to display numerous dysfunctional patterns in their social interactions with adults and peers, including both aggressiveness and withdrawal. Critical social skills instruction areas for abused children include interpersonal communication, problem-solving, self-control, appropriate assertiveness, and stress management.

4. Mental health disorders: Mental disorders in adolescents and adults appear to be strongly associated with, and exacerbated by, a lack of social competency and skill (Trower, Bryant, & Argyle, 1978; Kazdin, 1985). It is thought that the social inadequacy accompanying many mental disturbances results in increased social rejection and isolation, thus adding to the original sources of stress and deterioration. For example, adolescents in psychiatric settings have been found to be particularly deficient in conversation skills (Hansen, St. Lawrence, & Christoff, 1988). In addition, children who experience greater amounts of social isolation and rejection also are more likely to experience serious mental health problems in adulthood (Combs & Slaby, 1977).

5. Loneliness and despondency: A lack of age-appropriate social knowledge and the corresponding rejection by peers seem to be major factors associated with chronic loneliness, isolation, and periods of despondency in childhood and adolescence (Oden, 1980; LeCroy, 1983). Children lacking peer acceptance often are excluded from positive, friendly interactions with peers, and hence, a rich source of social learning and practice. Social skills training interventions have been demonstrated to decrease interpersonal loneliness, improve acceptance and inclusion by peers, and aid in the mainstreaming of handicapped children into regular education settings (Adams, Openshaw, Bennion, Mills, & Noble, 1988; Gresham, 1981).

6. Learning disabilities and school failure: While social skill deficits are not a casual factor in the presence of a learning handicap, they compound and intensify the difficulties encountered by learning-disabled children to a great degree (Cruickshank, Morse, & Johns, 1980; Hendrick, 1988). Learning-disabled children have difficulty interpreting and responding to social cues, discriminating situations, and fitting into social groups. The combination of a chronic learning handicap and social maladjustment can place a youth at risk for delinquency, school failure, chemical dependency, and serious mental health issues.

Deficits in social functioning appear to be implicated in numerous problem areas confronting children, adolescents, and young adults. The ability to interact effectively with others may be especially critical, though, during adolescence. This is normally a time when a youth would be refining a variety of basic social behaviors and learning more complex skills necessary for the transition to adulthood (LeCroy, 1983). Youth need to become increasingly skilled as they face the developmental tasks of adolescence, such as identity and value formation, independence from family, and appropriate group affiliation. Without a strong social and psychological base from which to develop, many adolescents fail to accomplish these tasks.

▶ Social skills and their components

The Boys Town Social Skills Curriculum is a catalog of 182 skills for successful interpersonal, emotional, and vocational functioning. The skills are drawn from the vast number of situational variables our young people may encounter as they grow and develop toward independence. Each skill has been task-analyzed into its essential behavioral elements that may include: 1) specific verbal responses; 2) nonverbal behaviors; 3) specific behaviors to omit; 4) metabehavioral cues and self-instructions; and, in some cases, 5) subclasses of skills that may be learned separately. The focus here is to construct a comprehensive treatment tool that is flexible and has a multitude of uses across numerous child-care and educational settings.

The skills contained in this curriculum are organized into four groups. They are grouped according to the perceived complexity associated with the performance of each skill, with the degree of difficulty increasing from Group 1 (Basic Skills) to Group 4 (Complex Skills). The nature of many of the component behaviors also changes with the increasing complexity. Complex Skills include skills that have several cognitive or metabehavioral steps, whereas Basic Skills include more basic curriculum content that matches the abilities of the participants.

In deciding which skills to target for a difficult youth problem or treatment issue, staff members should begin by analyzing the functional relationships that exist in the youth's environment that appear to reinforce the problem behavior. (See Chapter 5, "Principles of Behavior.") It also is critical to identify and target the specific situations and antecedent conditions in which the behavior occurs. Staff members then can begin the preventive measures that are discussed in Chapter 11, as well as systematically begin teaching appropriate alternative response sets (i.e. the individual skills listed in the curriculum). The staff must be sure, however, that the targeted skills will occur under the same situational variables that are associated with the problem behavior being treated.

A list of the Social Skills Curriculum's 182 skills follows. At the end of the list, the eight skills of the first group (Basic Skills) have been expanded to include their components, with rationales and helpful hints for each step. A complete listing of all 182 Social Skills and their components is contained in another Boys Town publication, *Teaching Social Skills to Youth: A Curriculum for Child-Care Providers* (Dowd & Tierney, 1992).

Boys Town Social Skills Curriculum

Basic skills group

Skill 1 Following Instructions

Skill 2 Accepting "No" Answers

Skill 3 Engaging in a Conversation

Skill 4 Greeting Others

Skill 5 Accepting Criticism

Skill 6 Disagreeing Appropriately

Skill 7 Showing Respect

Skill 8 Showing Sensitivity to Others

Intermediate skills group

Skill 9 Accepting Apologies from Others

Skill 10 Accepting Compliments

Skill 11 Accepting Consequences

Skill 12 Accepting Decisions of Authority

Skill 13 Acknowledging Others' Presence or Greetings

Skill 14 Anger Control Strategies

Skill 15 Answering the Telephone

Skill 16 Appropriate Appearance

Skill 17 Appropriate Voice Tone

Skill 18 Appropriate Word Choice

Skill 19 Asking for Help

Skill 20 Asking Questions

Skill 21 Asking for Clarification

Skill 22 Being on Time (Promptness)

Skill 23 Checking In (or Checking Back)

Skill 24 Completing Homework

Skill 25 Completing Tasks

Skill 26 Complying with Reasonable Requests

Skill 27 Contributing to Discussions (Joining in a Conversation)

Skill 28 Conversation Skills — Initiating

Skill 29 Conversation Skills — Maintaining

Skill 30 Conversation Skills — Closing

Skill 31 Correcting Another Person (or Giving Criticism)

Skill 32 Following Rules

Skill 33 Following Written Instructions

Skill 34 Getting Another Person's Attention

Skill 35 Getting the Teacher's Attention

Skill 36 Giving Compliments

Skill 37 Good Quality of Work

Skill 38 Ignoring Distractions by Others

Skill 39 Interrupting Appropriately

Skill 40 Introducing Others

Skill 41 Listening to Others

Skill 42 Making an Apology

Skill 43 Making a Request (Asking a Favor)

Skill 44 Making a Telephone Call

Skill 45 Offering Assistance or Help

Skill 46 Participating in Activities

Skill 47 Personal Hygiene

Skill 48 Positive Self-Statements

Skill 49 Positive Statements about Others

Skill 50 Refraining from Possessing Contraband or Drugs

Skill 51 Reporting Emergencies

Skill 52 Reporting Other Youths' Behavior (or Peer Reporting)

Skill 53 Resisting Peer Pressure

Skill 54 Saying Good-bye to Guests

Skill 55 Saying "No" Assertively

Skill 56 Seeking Positive Attention

Skill 57 Showing Appreciation

Skill 58 Showing Interest

Skill 59 Staying on Task

Skill 60 Structured Problem-Solving (**SODAS**)

Skill 61 Table Etiquette

Skill 62 Volunteering

Skill 63 Waiting Your Turn

Skill 64 Willingness to Try New Tasks

Advanced skills group

Skill 65 Accepting Help or Assistance

Skill 66 Accepting Defeat or Loss

Skill 67 Accepting Winning Appropriately

Skill 68 Analyzing Social Situations

Skill 69 Analyzing Skills Needed for Different Situations

Skill 70 Analyzing Tasks to Be Completed

Skill 71 Appropriate Clothing Choice

Skill 72 Being Prepared for Class

Skill 73 Borrowing from Others

Skill 74 Care of Others' Property

Skill 75 Care of Own Belongings

Skill 76 Choosing Appropriate Friends

Skill 77 Complying with School Dress Code

Complex skills group

Basic Skills For Youth

(Skills and Components)

Basic skill 1

Following instructions

Step 1. Look at the person.

Rationale: Looking at the person shows that you are paying attention.

Helpful hints:

- Look at the person as you would a friend.

- Don't stare, make faces, or roll your eyes.

- Look at the person throughout your conversation. Avoid being distracted.

- Looking at the person will help you understand his or her mood.

Step 2. Say "Okay."

Rationale: Saying "Okay" lets the person know you understand.

Helpful hints:

- Answer right away.

- Use a pleasant tone of voice.

- Speak clearly.

- Smile and nod your head (if it is appropriate to do so).

Step 3. Do the task immediately.

Rationale: You are more likely to remember exactly what you're supposed to do if you do it right away.

Helpful hints:

- Complete each step of the task.

- Stay on task. Don't let other things interfere.

- Do the best job you can.

- If you have problems, ask for help.

Step 4. Check back.

Rationale: Checking back lets the person know that you have followed the instruction.

Helpful hints:

- Tell the person you have finished as soon as you are done.

- Explain exactly what you did.

- Ask if the job was done correctly.

- Correct anything that needs to be done over.

Basic skill 2
Accepting "No" answers

Step 1. Look at the person.

Rationale: Looking at the person shows that you are paying attention.

Helpful hints:

- Don't stare or make faces.

- Don't look away.

- If you are upset, control your emotions. Try to relax and stay calm.

- Listening carefully will help you understand what the other person is saying.

Step 2. Say "Okay."

Rationale: Saying "Okay" lets the other person know that you understand.

Helpful hints:

- Answer right away.

- Speak clearly. Don't mumble.

- Don't sound angry or start to argue. That might lead to problems.

- Take a deep breath if you feel upset.

Step 3. Calmly ask for a reason if you really don't understand.

Rationale: It is important for youth, as they grow, to understand that there are reasons for being told "No."

Helpful hints:

- Don't ask for a reason every time or you will be viewed as a complainer.

- People will think you are serious about wanting to know a reason if you ask for one calmly.

- Don't keep asking for reasons after you receive one.

- Use what you learn in these situations in the future.

Step 4. If you disagree, bring it up later.

Rationale: If you disagree right away, you will appear to be arguing.

Helpful hints:

- Take some time to plan how you are going to approach the person who told you "No."

- Plan in advance what you are going to say.

- Accept the answer, even if it is still "No."

- Be sure to thank the person for listening.

Basic skill 3
Engaging in a conversation

Step 1. Look at the person.

Rationale: Looking at the person shows that you are paying attention and shows the person that you want to talk.

Helpful hints:

- Look at the person as you would a friend.

- Look at the person's face; this will help you understand that person's mood.

Step 2. Use a pleasant tone of voice.

Rationale: People won't want to talk to someone who seems unpleasant, angry, or threatening.

Helpful hints:

- Speak clearly.

- Use short sentences that are easily understood.

- Think before you speak.

Step 3. Ask the person questions.

Rationale: Asking questions includes the other person in the conversation.

Helpful hints:

- Avoid asking questions that can be answered with a "Yes" or a "No."

- Ask the person about his or her opinions, likes and dislikes, and interests.

- Listen intently.

- Be prepared to answer questions the person might ask you.

Step 4. Don't interrupt.

Rationale: Interrupting shows you don't care what the other person is saying.

Helpful hints:

- Make sure the person is done speaking before you respond.

- Maintain eye contact.

- Maintain good posture; don't distract the other person by fidgeting.

- Don't monopolize the conversation or jump from topic to topic.

Basic skill 4

Greeting others

Step 1. Look at the person and smile.

Rationale: Looking at the person and smiling is one way of showing that you really want to meet him or her.

Helpful hints:

- Get the person's attention appropriately.

- Don't stare or make faces.

- Look at the person as you would a friend. Don't force your smile.

- Smiling sets a friendly tone for the beginning of your conversation.

Step 2. Use a pleasant tone of voice.

Rationale: You will make a good impression if you appear to be friendly.

Helpful hints:

- Speak clearly.

- Talk loud enough to be heard, but not too loud.

- Use proper grammar and avoid slang words.

- Don't interrupt.

Step 3. State your own name.

Rationale: People need to know who you are if they want to talk to you.

Helpful hints:

- Wait for the right time to introduce yourself.

- Be confident when you introduce yourself.

- Share other information about yourself, if appropriate.

- Listen when the other person states his or her name.

Step 4. Shake the person's hand.

Rationale: Shaking hands is a traditional way of greeting someone.

Helpful hints:

- Use a firm grip, but don't squeeze too hard.

- Three shakes is about right when shaking hands.

- Say "It's nice to meet you" as you shake hands.

- Make sure your hand is clean before shaking hands with someone.

Step 5. When departing, again say "It was nice to meet you."

Rationale: Saying good-bye ends your conversation on a friendly note.

Helpful hints:

- Be sincere.

- Shake the person's hand again, if appropriate, when you leave.

- Use the person's name again when saying good-bye.

- Remember the person's name should you meet again.

Basic skill 5

Accepting criticism

Step 1. Look at the person.

Rationale: Looking at the person shows that you are paying attention.

Helpful hints:

- Don't stare or make faces.

- Look at the person throughout the conversation. Don't look away.

- Listen carefully and try not to be distracted.

- Paying attention shows courtesy; looking away shows disinterest.

Step 2. Say "Okay."

Rationale: Saying "Okay" shows that you understand what the other person is saying.

Helpful hints:

- Nodding your head also shows that you understand.

- Don't mumble.

- By nodding your head or saying "Okay" frequently throughout a long conversation, you let the speaker know that you are still listening carefully.

- Use a pleasant tone of voice. Don't be sarcastic.

Step 3. Don't argue.

Rationale: Accepting criticism without arguing shows that you are mature.

Helpful hints:

- Stay calm.

- Try to learn from what the person is saying so you can do a better job next time.

- Remember that the person who is giving you criticism is only trying to help.

- If you disagree, wait until later to discuss the matter.

Basic skill 6
Disagreeing appropriately

Step 1. Look at the person.

Rationale: Looking at the person shows that you are paying attention.

Helpful hints:

- Don't stare or make faces.

- Keep looking at the person throughout your conversation.

- Be pleasant and smile.

- Look at the person as you would a friend.

Step 2. Use a pleasant tone of voice.

Rationale: The person is more likely to listen to you if you use a pleasant tone of voice.

Helpful hints:

- Speak slowly and clearly. Don't mumble.

- Use short sentences. They are easily understood.

- Keep a comfortable distance between you and the other person while you are talking.

- Smile. People are more comfortable talking with someone who is friendly.

Step 3. Make an empathy/concern statement.

Rationale: Using a statement of empathy or concern gets the conversation off to a positive start.

Helpful hints:

- Plan what you are going to say before you start to speak.

- If you still feel uneasy about how you are going to start your conversation, practice.

- Start to discuss your concerns as part of a conversation, not a confrontation.

- Be sincere.

Step 4. Be specific when telling why you disagree.

Rationale: Using vague words can lead to confusion and doesn't get your point across.

Helpful hints:

- Use as much detailed information as possible.

- Be prepared to back up what you say.

- If necessary, practice what you are going to say.

- Always remember to think before you speak.

Step 5. Give a rationale.

Rationale: Your disagreement will carry more weight if you give a valid reason.

Helpful hints:

- Be sure that your rationales make sense.

- Support your rationales with facts and details.

- One or two rationales are usually enough.

- Remember to stay calm during the conversation.

Step 6. Say "Thank you."

Rationale: Saying "Thank you" shows that you appreciate the person taking the time to listen to you.

Helpful hints:

- Remember to say "Thank you" even if you didn't get the response you wanted.

- Be sincere.

- Being polite makes it more likely that the person will listen to you again.

- Saying "Thank you" ends the conversation on a positive note.

Basic skill 7
Showing respect

Step 1. Obey a request to stop a negative behavior.

Rationale: When you obey a request to stop a negative behavior, you show that you can follow instructions. Being able to follow instructions is one form of showing respect.

Helpful hints:

- By stopping your negative behavior, you may avoid getting into trouble.

- There will always be people who have authority over you. You must do what they say.

Step 2. Refrain from teasing, threatening, or making fun of others.

Rationale: By refraining from such behaviors, it shows you understand that teasing, threatening, and making fun can be hurtful to others.

Helpful hints:

- If you are always making fun of people or threatening them, you won't have many friends.

- People will think of you only as a tease, not as a nice person.

Step 3. Allow others to have their privacy.

Rationale: Sometimes people need or want to be alone. You show respect by adhering to their wishes.

Helpful hints:

- Always knock before entering someone's room or a room with a closed door.

- Honor someone's desire to be left alone.

Step 4. Obtain permission before using another person's property.

Rationale: You have certain possessions that are very important to you. You don't want people using them without permission. When you ask permission to use others' things, you show that same kind of respect.

Helpful hints:

- Always return items in the same condition as when you borrowed them.

- If you damage a borrowed item, offer to repair or replace it.

Step 5. Do not damage or vandalize public property.

Rationale: Vandalism and damaging property are against the law. Besides getting into trouble, you show disrespect for your community and country when you vandalize public property.

Helpful hints:

- Accidents do happen, but they always should be reported.

- Offer to replace or repair property you have damaged.

Step 6. Refrain from conning or persuading others into breaking rules.

Rationale: People will think less of you if you are always trying to take advantage of others or get them into trouble.

Helpful hints:

- If you use people, they won't trust you.

- People don't appreciate being manipulated.

Step 7. Avoid acting obnoxiously in public.

Rationale: You make a good impression with people when you show that you know how to behave and use proper social skills in public.

Helpful hints:

- Be on your best behavior in public. That means don't do such things as curse, swear, spit, and belch.

- Be courteous to others and mind your manners.

Step 8. Dress appropriately when in public.

Rationale: When in public, people are expected to look their best. When you live up to this expectation, you show that you are mature and understand society's rules.

Helpful hints:

- Being well-groomed and well-dressed makes a good impression.

- Use good judgment when deciding what to wear. Where you are going usually dictates what you wear.

Basic skill 8
Showing sensitivity to others

Step 1. Express interest and concern for others, especially when they are having troubles.

Rationale: If you help others, they are more likely to help you.

Helpful hints:

- If you see someone in trouble, ask if you can help.

- Sometimes, just showing you care is enough to help a person get through a difficult time.

Step 2. Recognize that disabled people deserve the same respect as anyone else.

Rationale: A disability does not make a person inferior. Helping people with disabilities without ridiculing or patronizing them shows that you believe all people are equal, although some people may need a little extra assistance.

Helpful hints:

- Be ready to help a disabled person when needed by doing such things as holding open a door, carrying a package, or giving up your seat.

- Don't stare at disabled people or make comments about their special needs.

Step 3. Apologize or make amends for hurting someone's feelings or causing harm.

Rationale: Saying you're sorry shows that you can take responsibility for your actions and can admit when you've done something wrong.

Helpful hints:

- You can harm someone by what you fail to do, just as easily as by what you do. Some examples are breaking a promise or not sticking up for someone who is being picked on.

- If you hurt someone, apologize immediately and sincerely.

Step 4. Recognize that people of different races, religions, and backgrounds deserve to be treated the same way as you would expect to be treated.

Rationale: Treating others equally shows that although people are different, you believe that it shouldn't matter in the way you treat them.

Helpful hints:

- Don't make jokes and rude comments about the color of someone's skin or what he or she believes.

• Some people have different customs for doing things. Some people have more money than others. No matter, all people should be treated the same.

▶ Summary

All young people need a repertoire of social skills in order to interact with others in socially acceptable ways and to make appropriate decisions in social situations. This is even more true for youth who have been taught inappropriate ways of getting their needs met. The philosophy and methods of the Boys Town Family Home Program are directed at teaching youth, in a family setting, the essential life skills they need for a successful transition to young adulthood.

The Boys Town Social Skills Curriculum comprises 182 skills that are divided into four categories, based on their perceived complexity: Basic Skills, Intermediate Skills, Advanced Skills, and Complex Skills. Each skill is broken down into component steps that include specific verbal responses, nonverbal behaviors, behaviors that should be omitted, cues and self-instructions, and in some cases, subclasses of skills that can be learned separately. These skills form the cornerstone of treatment in Boys Town programs, and are taught so that youth can replace inappropriate behaviors with those that are appropriate.

▶ Model comparisons

In comparing the six treatment theories in the area of social skills, the modalities seem equally divided. Only three models — Behavioral, Eclectic, and Boys Town — have at least some form of skill development. The others — Psychodynamic (Medical), Cognitive, and Positive Peer Culture — offer treatment that is based on a discussion of thoughts or feelings rather than on behavior or skill acquisition.

In the Psychodynamic (Medical) Model, the primary focus is on reanalyzing past events and the child's feelings about them. The goal is to change the child's feelings about these events so he or she would feel and react differently in the future.

The Cognitive Model has similar goals, but probably attempts to achieve them by having the child reenact similar situations, moving closer and closer to reality with each reenactment. The goal is to have the child change his or her feelings about the real situation while moving closer to it.

In a program using Positive Peer Culture, the focus would be similar. To achieve the desired goal, the peer group confronts the child about his or her thoughts or feelings about situations.

All three of the other programs would use some level of skill development. How this is used, and how much emphasis is placed on it, varies from program to program.

The focus of the Behavioral Model is on shaping the child's behavior until it is socially appropriate. This is accomplished by altering the stimuli in the environment. Since the child is only passively involved in this process, the skills do not always seem natural and the child is not always aware that he or she is acquiring new skills.

The behavior management portion of the eclectic-based program developed by the University of Oklahoma is based on learning theory, and there is an expectation for skill development. The model provides an explanation of the theory behind the shaping and changing of behavior, and mentions the most basic of skills. Since only a limited range of behaviors for the child to learn is provided, the individual child-care worker must decide what skills should be taught. The model does not specifically describe the steps that are required to perform the skills, which could make it difficult for the child to learn them. These factors could make it difficult to replicate this model across programs, or across staffs within programs.

The Boys Town Model also is based on learning theory. The program has a clearly defined curriculum of skills for children to learn, and these all have been task-analyzed and broken down into specific behaviors. Since the program actively involves the child in the treatment process, he or she is very aware of the skills that are being developed and the reasons for learning them. Since the program has a clearly defined curriculum, it is easily duplicated in different circumstances or settings.

CHAPTER THREE

Relationship development

Most of the youth who enter residential care facilities have had difficulty developing positive relationships. They have had difficulty making and keeping friends, and also have had problems developing relationships with adults in authority, such as parents, teachers, and employers. Yet, nurturing relationships are a key to living a rewarding and happy life. Positive relationships between child-care workers and the youth they work with are critical for the youth if they are to benefit from their treatment experiences.

This section will explore the benefits of strong relationship development in residential care facilities, and present several techniques for enhancing relationship development.

▶ Benefits of building strong relationships

There are numerous benefits to developing and maintaining strong, personal relationships with each youth in a residential care facility. In general, strong relationships between you and the youth enhance your ability to effect change in each youth's life, create a more pleasant living environment, and improve the effectiveness of the overall program. Strong relationships contribute substantially to your ability to help each youth learn and grow. When relationships are healthy and strong, youth are more likely to spend time with the child-care workers. When youth seek you out and want to be with you, the entire teaching and learning process is enhanced. You will have more opportunities to teach by example as youth spend more time in the presence of positive, adult role models.

Furthermore, as relationships develop, the youth are more likely to identify with and accept the values, rationales, and opinions you express. Research shows that youth are more likely to emulate the behaviors, values, and morals of adults with whom they have good relationships.

Not only is the effectiveness of role-modeling improved due to good relationships, but the youth's receptivity to direct teaching also is improved. That is, youth are more likely to accept your feedback, whether it takes the form of praise for appropriate behavior or teaching to correct an inappropriate behavior. They can be taught crucial skills like following instructions or accepting criticism more readily. Such skills not only help the youth learn other skills (i.e. you have to be able to follow instructions and accept criticism before you can be taught other skills), but also enhance the general pleasantness of the environment.

The youth who enter residential care facilities need not only the benefit of positive role models and active help through teaching, but also need to be able to talk with child-care staff members about how they are feeling and what they are thinking. With sensitive relationships to rely on, the youth are much more likely to communicate frequently and honestly. Frequent, open communication allows you to be more sensitive to the needs of each youth, and increases your ability to individualize the program to best help the youth.

Relationship development also positively affects some critical youth behaviors. Youth who feel positive about their treatment and the child-care staff are less likely to run away, and are more likely to return if they should run away. The more closely the youth identify with you, the less likely they are to be negatively influenced by their peers. Youth who feel close to you are more likely to resist drugs, illegal activity, and acts of defiance. In addition, youth who identify closely with you are more likely to speak positively about you to others, and speak positively about the residential program in general.

As youth develop close ties with you, they begin to care about your opinions of them. In essence, your approval and perception of the youth become reinforcers for them. Over time, youth come to care about the opinions and want the approval of other important role models and significant others such as teachers, parents, etc. The more youth value these relationships, the more likely they are to continue behaving in appropriate ways after leaving the care facility.

▶ How relationships develop

Relationships do not develop over the course of a few days or even months, nor can a relationship ever be considered fully "developed." Rather, a relationship can be viewed as continually developing over time, across the events and issues that arise as people interact with one another. Relationships, positive or negative, begin to develop as a result of people interacting with others around common experiences or interests. Strong, positive relationships grow because people have mutually enjoyable or compatible behaviors, qualities, or values.

Generally speaking, there is a common set of behaviors and attitudes related to relationship development that are both acceptable in society and generally valued by members of society. These behaviors and values include such concepts as honesty, sensitivity, concern for others, a sense of humor, reliability, willingness to listen etc. In essence, these behaviors and values can be conceptualized as skills that help build positive relationships. With these skills, people begin to develop positive relationships with one another.

How to assess relationships

Even though you are helping youth learn how to develop positive relationships by teaching important skills, assessing the relationship development between you and the youth is essential. When a relationship is weak, you should request feedback from other staff members to help you strengthen the relationship.

Here are ways to determine whether a relationship is strong or weak.

Strong relationship

1. The youth spends a lot of his or her free time around child-care staff members.

2. The youth engages in behaviors that he or she knows please the staff (e.g. says "Please" and "Thank you" to staff members, gives staff members birthday cards).

3. The youth volunteers to help staff members in some way even though no rewards are associated with the volunteering.

4. The youth routinely makes positive com-

ments about the staff members to other youth and adults.

Weak relationship

1. The youth spends little or none of his or her free time around staff members.

2. The youth usually fails to engage in behaviors that he or she knows please the staff.

3. The youth volunteers to help staff members and volunteers only when he or she knows there will be a reward for volunteering.

4. The youth routinely makes negative or inappropriate comments about staff members to other youth and adults.

Quality components: Skills that help develop relationships

Although teaching procedures such as Effective Praise® (Chapter 9) and Preventive Teaching® (Chapter 11) can build relationships, their use does not guarantee that strong relationships will develop. Teaching components must be accompanied by quality components as well.

Quality components refer to positive verbal and nonverbal behaviors that accompany the use of the procedural components. Quality components include looking at the youth, answering the youth's questions, having a pleasant facial expression, appropriately using humor, appropriately using physical contact such as hugs or an arm around the shoulder, etc. Research conducted by Willner, Braukmann, Kirigin, Fixsen, Phillips, & Wolf (1975) indicated that youth can clearly describe staff behaviors they like and dislike, and supported the importance of quality components in relationship development. The lists below include some of these behaviors.

Liked Behaviors
Calm, pleasant voice tone
Offering or providing help
Joking
Positive feedback
Fairness
Explanation of how or what to do
Explanation of why (giving reasons)
Enthusiasm
Politeness
Getting right to the point
Smiling

Disliked Behaviors
Describing only what the child did wrong

Anger
Negative feedback
Profanity
Lack of understanding
Unfriendly
Unpleasant
Bad attitude
Unpleasant physical contact
Mean, insulting remarks
Not providing opportunities to speak
Shouting
Accusing, blaming statements
Throwing objects

▶ Helping youth learn how to develop relationships

For the most part, boys and girls who are placed in residential care facilities have not yet developed positive relationship-building skills because of poor role models, damaged learning histories, or simply because they have not had anyone to guide them through a particular phase of development. Some youth are less "likeable" than others. They need to have certain skills that make them more socially attractive to others. It is your responsibility to teach the youth the skills they need to develop positive relationships with adults and peers. Some of these skills are listed below.

Express appreciation — The youth is able to thank individuals for their assistance, helpful suggestions, expressing interest, and any aid others have provided or offered to provide.

Express compliments — The youth is able to acknowledge the accomplishments and well-being of others.

Accept compliments — The youth is able to look at the person giving the compliment and offer an expression of appreciation for the compliment.

Accept criticism — The youth is able to look at the person giving the criticism, acknowledge the criticism, correct the problem, and check back with the person after the problem is corrected.

Converse with others — The youth is able to look at the person speaking, respond when spoken to in a manner that expresses concern or interest, and ask relevant questions about the person or conversation topic.

When teaching youth relationship-building skills, it is especially important to apply the concepts of each teaching procedure (see Chapter 9, "Effective Praise," Chapter 10, "Corrective Teaching/The Teaching Interaction®," and Chapter 11, "Preventive Teaching") and maintain consistent tolerance levels. (See Chapter 4, "Tolerance Levels.")

For example, you should be pleasant when teaching relationship-building skills, and should model these skills when interacting with other adults and youth (e.g. giving youth compliments). Also, you should correct a youth when he or she fails to use a positive relationship-building skill that has been taught, or fails to perform the relationship-building skill to criteria. By effectively combining and putting these concepts into practice, you help youth learn to develop relationships, and directly affect your own ability to develop a solid, positive relationship with each youth.

▶ Other elements of a positive relationship

There are a number of other activities and behaviors that you can engage in to help build relationships with your youth. Spending time in recreational activities, talking together, attending events, or working alongside the youth (e.g. homework, arts and crafts, etc.) provides valuable opportunities for you to get to know your youngsters.

Because shared experiences and "remember when" times are important for relationship development, there are times when participation in activities and events should not depend on whether the youth has access to privileges. You and your youth should plan and participate in recreational activities approximately two to four times each month. Such activities might include playing video games, roller skating, seeing movies, etc. Planning and celebrating holidays and birthdays provide special opportunities to develop close relationships. Attending these activities with your youth is imperative because you can enjoy each other's company outside the daily program structure.

You also develop close relationships by displaying concern for the happiness and well-being of each youth. This means using Preventive Teaching with each youth to see that he or she has the necessary skills to get his or her needs met. You advocate for each youth to see that second (or even third and fourth) chances are granted. You are there to listen when a youth needs to talk, are sensitive to the youth's feelings and background, and are appropriately affectionate with the youth.

In the midst of the structure provided by the program, there is room for and a need for flexibility as well. You need to ask your youth for input, allow them to help plan activities, and be open to their concerns and criticism.

Spending time with youngsters, enjoying activities, displaying concern, and demonstrating flexibility go a long way toward building relationships, relationships that grow stronger day to day, and last long after a youth leaves the care facility.

Finally, relationship development is an important part of dealing with problem behavior. Even when dealing with serious misbehavior (see Chapter 12, "Intensive Teaching"), you use large amounts of empathy and praise to maintain and continue to develop positive relationships.

Summary

Positive relationships between child-care workers and the youth are critical if the youth are to benefit from their treatment experiences. Strong relationships enhance a child-care worker's ability to bring about change in the youth's lives, create a more pleasant living environment, and improve the effectiveness of the program.

Relationships between child-care workers and their youth are continually developing. Youth who feel positive about their treatment are less likely to run away and are more likely to work hard to earn the approval of the child-care workers.

Quality components also are important to relationship development. Quality components are the verbal and non-verbal behaviors that accompany the use of procedural components. They can include looking at a youth, having a pleasant facial expression, and using appropriate physical contact such as hugs to show affection.

Model comparisons

As we look at the six models we are comparing, relationship development certainly is an area where we see differences. Every program except the Behavior Model requires some form of relationship between the professional and the child, but the level and meaning of this relationship can vary greatly.

When looking at the Psycho-dynamic (Medical) Model, it is apparent that if the therapist's goal is to have children trace

their developmental lines through analysis and recollection, then the majority of the children would have to form some sort of relationship with the therapist in order to be comfortable doing this. Most children have to feel a certain level of trust with someone before they share intimate past experiences, and this normally is based on the type of relationship they have with that other person. Since this form of therapy typically takes place in a formal setting, in short sessions once or twice a week, the depth of that relationship could be somewhat limited.

This also would be the case in the Cognitive Model. Although the child would typically have to develop a relationship of trust with the therapist, the setting — although perhaps not quite as formal — again limits the amount of time the therapist is able to spend with the child.

In either case, this does not in anyway mean that the relationship is not important or would not have a positive impact on the child; it only means that there are others who are spending much more time with the child. These people have the potential to form much deeper relationships.

In the Behavioral Model, relationship development is not a necessary component of the therapy. Since the behaviorist is typically focused on changing the stimuli in the environment, he or she would not have to build any special bond with the child in order to do this. The only exception would be a situation in which the behaviorist was attempting to use himself or herself as a reinforcer for the child. Normally, however, consequences and antecedents could change without a behaviorist-child relationship, and without the child even being aware of what the behaviorist is trying to accomplish.

The Boys Town Model, although based on learning theory, makes relationship-building an extremely important facet of the treatment program. One of the main goals of the program is to help the child learn socially appropriate behavior so he or she can develop relationships with others. Since the caregivers are implementing the program, providing all of the child's primary needs, and spending the most time with the child, they have the opportunity to develop very deep and bonding relationships with the child. The program also provides the child-care worker with very specific skills for building relationships and a clear process for teaching these to the child. Because the children spend the majority of their time with the child-care workers, they have many opportunities to practice these relationship-building skills. The child-care workers also have many opportunities to reinforce the child for using these behaviors. When the child-care workers are implementing the program and teaching these skills, they want the child to be actively involved in the treatment. The stronger the relationship between the caregivers and the youth, the more apt the child is to cooperate in the treatment and to want to change his or her behavior.

Strong relationships are emphasized in the eclectic-based University of Oklahoma program as well. Again, because the caregiver is the primary treatment agent, the opportunity for strong relationship development is there. Many different theoretical ideas regarding relationship-building are shared. Unfortunately, this program does not

provide a clear structure for teaching the child relationship-building skills. This could possibly lead to situations where the child engages in inappropriate behaviors, and the child-care worker does not know how to teach alternative behaviors. These types of situations could damage the relationship between the child and the child-care worker.

In Positive Peer Culture, relationship-building would be an asset as well. Normally, the youth has to develop some level of trust with his or her peers for this model to be successful, since it is based on having the child discuss his or her thoughts and feelings with other youth.

However, since the nature of these interactions is often confrontational, developing positive relationships may sometimes be difficult. Consider this potential problem: A child begins to feel that he or she can trust the other youth and becomes willing to share his or her feelings with them. If the child is immediately involved in a confrontation, he or she may be less willing to share feelings in the future. If the staff members who are implementing the program are not aware of this situation, it could be difficult to accomplish the program's goals.

CHAPTER FOUR

Tolerance levels

Generally, tolerance is regarded as a positive quality in which a person is open to and accepting of a wide variety of beliefs, ideas, and differences among people. When speaking of tolerance in terms of behaviors, however, there is a fine line — or tolerance level — that separates the behaviors a person will or will not accept as appropriate. In the Boys Town Family Home Program, tolerance levels determine when staff members should use Effective Praise interactions (Chapter 9) to reward appropriate behaviors or Teaching Interactions (Chapter 10) to correct inappropriate behaviors.

A high tolerance level means that a great deal of inappropriate behavior is accepted or tolerated; a low tolerance level means that very little inappropriate behavior is accepted or tolerated. It is critical for child-care workers to know that they can maintain low tolerance levels and still build positive relationships. Raising tolerance levels will not help build relationships, and will not help the youth learn the skills they need to develop positive relationships.

In many residential programs, tolerance levels are very high for a variety of reasons. First, child-care workers might excuse misbehavior in an effort to be sympathetic and understanding of the problems the youth have faced. Some residential programs believe that there are limits to how much a youth can learn given his or her background, social disabilities, learning disabilities, etc.

Another reason that tolerance levels are high in some residential programs is that the principles of behavior are at work.

That is, youth teach the child-care workers not to deal directly with problem behaviors. When staff members directly address problem behaviors, they are often met with increasingly defiant youth behavior. In essence, the youth in the program have effectively punished staff members for addressing problem behavior. As a result, the staff begins to ignore all but the most blatant inappropriate behavior in hopes that it will "go away." Instead, small behaviors escalate as the youth attempt to determine the limits that have been set. This pattern of antecedents, behavior, and consequences is logical when child-care workers do not have the knowledge and skill to deal with problems effectively.

▶ **Importance of low tolerances**

Inappropriate behavior is a sign that a youth does not know the appropriate behavior or skill to use in a given situation (e.g. the youth does not know the skill of "Accepting Criticism"). As a child-care worker, it is your responsibility to teach these skills when inappropriate behavior occurs. Low tolerances are important if youth are to learn the critical skills they need for success after leaving the program. By tolerating inappropriate behavior, the child-care staff sends a message to the youth that such behavior is acceptable. The acceptance of problem behaviors inadvertently reinforces and strengthens those behaviors. At best, the youth is confused about what is and what is not acceptable. At worst, failure to teach more appropriate skills means that youth are "set up" for failure in other settings since other adults in authority may not tolerate such problem behavior. In effect, the youth are placed at greater risk when tolerance levels are high.

When a child-care staff maintains low tolerances, youth have a clearer picture of what is expected of them. The staff should strive for consistency in responding to the youth's appropriate or inappropriate behaviors. Consistency reduces youth confusion, defines expectations, and makes it easier for youth to learn and maintain appropriate skills. Consistency also will help decrease the likelihood of tension and/or conflict between staff members and youth. The youth will perceive the staff as being more fair and reasonable, and positive relationships are more likely to develop and grow. By frequently talking to each other about youth progress and by discussing any inconsistencies, staff members can work toward more consistent (equal), fair tolerance levels.

▶ **Communicating tolerance levels**

From the moment a youth enters a residential care facility until the day he or she leaves, the child-care workers will have numerous opportunities to communicate their tolerance levels to the youth. The Boys Town Family Home Program teaching procedures (see Chapters 9, 10, 11, and 12) provide staff members with specific, effective means of communicating tolerance levels by emphasizing the importance of being pleasant, positive, and specific when interacting with youth.

Child-care workers also communicate their tolerance levels through their own behavior or modeling. For example, when a staff member greets a visitor, he or she is providing the youth with a behavioral example of the tolerance levels for greeting visitors. If staff members expect youth to shake hands with visitors, they should model handshaking when they greet visitors. By modeling the appropriate behavior, staff members increase the likelihood that youth will engage in the expected, desirable behavior.

A general rule of thumb regarding tolerance levels is to expect socially appropriate behavior from each and every youth. That is, the staff should not excuse a youth's inappropriate behavior because of his or her background, referral reasons, or behavior pattern. To expect anything less than appropriate behavior creates "institutional tolerance levels" — behaviors that are inappropriate in society at large but permitted in an institutional setting. Youth need to engage in normal, socially accepted behaviors to succeed outside of any program. To bring about behavior change, organizations must provide an environment where tolerance levels match or exceed those of society at large.

▶ Determining the appropriateness of behavior

Before staff members can adequately communicate their tolerance levels, they must develop a way to determine the appropriateness of youth behavior. The ability to recognize and specifically describe verbal and nonverbal behaviors (see Chapter 7,

"Recognizing and Describing Behavior") is critical in making this determination.

Here are some factors that determine the appropriateness of youth behavior:

Factor: Conflicts with social norms.
Example: Vandalizing a pop machine.

Factor: Breaks a rule in the program.
Example: Not making the bed before going to school.

Factor: Causes physical harm to any living being.
Example: Kicking or hitting a peer.

Factor: Results in an extreme emotional outburst.
Example: Screaming at the child-care staff.

Factor: Causes discomfort or embarrassment to others.
Example: Swearing at the child-care staff in a public setting.

Factor: Leads to negative consequences.
Example: Damaging property.

Factor: Is not appropriate for the situation.
Example: Wearing cut-offs and a T-shirt to school.

As you and other staff members set expectations for your youth, you also need to understand how patience, encouragement, and recognition are combined with low tolerances to support the youth as they learn new ways of thinking and behaving. That is, you need to have low tolerances and high expectations, but also recognize and praise the youth for any positive behavioral changes or efforts made to master new skills. Low tolerances do not ensure rapid changes in youth behavior. However, low tolerances help staff members to effectively and consistently communicate what skills they expect the youth to learn and use. Even though the youth may fall short of the staff's expectations, any efforts the youth make toward those expectations need to be praised, encouraged, and rewarded.

▶ Summary

Tolerance, in behavioral terms, refers to the types of behaviors a person will or will not accept as appropriate. A high tolerance level allows a lot of inappropriate behavior to occur. A low tolerance level means that little inappropriate behavior is accepted. The Boys Town Family Home Program stresses the use of low tolerance levels when working with troubled youth. This gives youth a clearer picture of what is expected of them, and discourages youth from engaging in inappropriate behaviors. Child-care workers also must realize that they can maintain low tolerances and still build strong relationships with their youth.

It also is important to respond to youth behavior in a consistent manner. That is, respond the same way each time a youth displays a specific behavior. Consistency reduces youth confusion and makes it easier for the youth to learn appropriate skills.

▶ Model comparisons

When we refer to tolerance or tolerance levels in this chapter, we are referring to that line that distinguishes appropriate

behavior from inappropriate behavior. So if someone has low tolerances, he or she would not "tolerate" very much in the way of inappropriate behavior. Typically, this would be paired with high expectations for appropriate behavior. It is important to note that what we expect of a child is often what we get.

When looking at the Psychodynamic (Medical) Model, one could assume that it would allow for a high tolerance. There could be several reasons for this. First, the therapist spends such a limited amount of time with the child that he or she could "tolerate" much more inappropriate behavior than someone who's spending a great deal of time with the child. Another reason would be that due to the nature of the program, with the child talking and expressing many feelings, it often is felt that it is normal or okay to display inappropriate behavior. So, for example, if a child is in the therapist's office displaying aggressive behavior, such as shouting, cursing, or making threats, the therapist might say it's okay because this resulted from the feelings the child was remembering.

We would probably see the same type of situation in the Cognitive Model, except that the child may be encouraged to turn that aggressive behavior toward some object as a way of building toward reality. Again, the behavior probably would be considered acceptable since the child is just "acting out" his or her feelings, and once the feelings change, the behavior will probably go away. The problem with this is that it may be telling the child that it's okay to act that way.

In the Behavioral Model, the behaviorist probably would set a low tolerance level since the goal is to change socially unacceptable behaviors and increase acceptable behaviors. In setting a low tolerance, however, it usually is important to have a good relationship with the child. When low tolerances are paired with warmth and caring, the child sees the adult as someone who is truly concerned about him or her. Since the behaviorist does not typically build a relationship with the child, this may not be important.

In the Boys Town Model, the child-care worker is asked to develop a low tolerance. We feel that the child needs to understand that caregivers will not tolerate unacceptable behavior, and that they have high expectations for appropriate behavior. Children want adults to set clear limits and expectations for them. By doing this, the child-care worker helps to establish a relationship with the child. This is done with a great deal of praise, warmth, and concern for the child, so that he or she clearly understands that the caregivers are interested in the child and are there to help. Since the children are actively involved in the treatment process, they often develop these same expectations for themselves. Since most of society has a low tolerance for inappropriate behavior, this helps to set up the children for success in other situations.

The University of Oklahoma's eclectic-based program stresses the importance of setting appropriate and clear expectations. It provides clear examples of inappropriate expectations and reasons for not engaging in this behavior. The program, however, does not clearly define alternative behaviors. Therefore, the child-care staff could have low tolerances and high expectations, but the children may not understand how to meet them.

Tolerances typically are not taught or clearly defined in a Positive Peer Culture. This could result in different expectations for each group of youngsters. There also is a risk that expectations set by certain peers will be unrealistic and possibly unchallenged. Certain rules and expectations may be set for the particular setting the child is in, but these may or may not be transferable to other settings. This could make it difficult for a child to learn realistic expectations and generalize these to other situations.

CHAPTER FIVE

Principles of behavior

In order to change behavior, child-care workers need to have a basic knowledge of how behavior is learned. This chapter is designed to acquaint you with certain behavioral principles that affect how behavior is learned, and to specify the relationship between behavior and the conditions surrounding the behavior.

Behavioral principles are the fundamental laws or assumptions concerning the nature of behavior. They specify the relationships between behavior and the specific circumstances surrounding the behavior. Some principles of behavior are especially important for child-care workers whose task is to change behaviors. For instance, you can use the principle of positive reinforcement to increase appropriate behaviors and the principle of response cost to decrease inappropriate behavior. You also can use processes called generalization and discrimination to bring behavior under the control of appropriate antecedent events. Used together, these principles enable child-care workers to help youth by changing their behavior.

▶ Positive reinforcement

Positive reinforcement means providing positive consequences immediately after a behavior to increase the likelihood that the behavior will occur again in the future. Positive consequences "reinforce" a behavior (i.e. make it stronger), and positive reinforcement can occur with natural consequences or applied consequences (e.g. points or tokens). Positive reinforcement is used to increase or maintain appropriate behavior.

These are some of the factors that determine the effectiveness of positive reinforcement:

1. Choosing the right reinforcer. Reinforcers need to be individualized so that they actually do bring about behavior change. (See the "Categories of Reinforcers" list below.) Of course, the way you can tell whether a positive consequence is a real reinforcer is to observe its effect on the youngster's behavior. If the behavior increases or improves, you chose the right reinforcer. Child-care workers can use the "Reward Survey" to help them determine individual reinforcers for a youth.

Categories of reinforcers

Consumable — snacks, candy, juice, meals out, etc.

Activity — watching TV, reading books, hobbies, movies, sports, putting make-up on, styling hair, etc.

Manipulative — toys, blocks, puzzles, games, models, painting kits, etc.

Possessional — awards, special books, magazines, objects for collecting, clothes, etc.

Social — (Verbal) "good job," "good girl," praise and compliments, etc.; (Physical) hugs, pats, winks, etc.

Exchange — stickers, stars, points, money, or other objects that can be exchanged for other reinforcers.

Reward survey

Fill out this reward survey for a youth. Use the information when you want to provide rewards and positive consequences for the youth's appropriate behavior.

People — Who does the youth like to spend time with?

Everyday activities — What everyday activities does the youth like to do (e.g. play Monopoly, roller-skate, watch TV, play with puzzles, dolls, trucks)?

Special activities — What special activities does the youth enjoy (e.g. going to movies or zoo, baking cookies, going to a baseball game)?

Foods — What are the youth's favorite foods and beverages?

Attention — What specific kinds of verbal and physical attention from you and others does the youth like (e.g. praise, compliments, hugs, pats on the back)?

Exchange rewards — What kind of exchange rewards (e.g. stars, tokens, money, happy faces) does the youth like to receive?

Other rewards — List anything the youth likes, is interested in, spends time doing, or would like to spend more time doing.

2. Deliver the reinforcer immediately. To be most effective, reinforcers need to be given immediately after the behavior that you want to reinforce. As the amount of time between the occurrence of the behavior and the delivery of the consequence increases, the reinforcer's effectiveness in strengthening behavior decreases. Reinforcers are more effective when a youth receives them immediately for an appropriate behavior. Points or tokens can be given immediately after any behavior and later exchanged for the real, or "back-up," reinforcers of privileges.

3. Choose the right amount or size. The size of the reinforcer should fit the behavior. The longer a behavior takes to learn, the newer the behavior is for a youth, or the more difficult it is, the larger the reward should be. Staff members may give a new youth lots of points for attending school for an entire week (e.g. the first time in three semesters), but give another youth, who has never had difficulty attending school, only a few points for near-perfect attendance over an entire nine-week period. You can tell if you have chosen the right amount by observing the behavior of the youth. If behavior is improving or positive behavior is being maintained, you have chosen correctly.

Fitting the consequence to the behavior

Factors to consider when deciding the amount or size of a positive consequence:

Difficulty of skill for the child

Time required to complete the skill

Situational circumstances

Youth's social history

---

4. Use reinforcers contingently. The easiest way to understand a contingency is to think of it as an "if ... then" situation. If the youth does the behavior, then he or she gets the consequence. Obtaining the consequence depends upon performing the behavior first. Staff members should always make positive consequences contingent upon positive behavior. Negative behavior should be analyzed to determine whether access to any possible contingent rewards may be reinforcing that behavior. For instance, you could inadvertently reinforce whining by giving a youth attention or by giving a youth something he or she wants.

5. Vary the use of reinforcers. If particular consequences are used too much they can lose their effectiveness. One piece of candy can be a reinforcer, but a whole bag of candy may lead to satiation and not be as reinforcing. Allowing a youth to watch a 30-minute show on TV may be a reinforcer, but allowing the youth to watch TV for three hours may not be. The concept of satiation also means that reinforcers are used when they are most in demand. Access to snacks an hour before dinner is much more reinforcing than snacks an hour after dinner. TV time when the latest rock video is on is more reinforcing than TV time when the news is on. You can maximize the effectiveness of positive consequences by using a variety of reinforcers and by using those that are most in demand by a youngster at the moment.

6. Use schedules of reinforcement. There are two basic schedules used to deliver reinforcers to youngsters. One is a continuous schedule, where a reinforcer is provided every time a target behavior occurs. A continuous schedule is very useful when teaching a new behavior. Reinforcing a youngster each and every time a new behavior is performed strengthens and encourages that behavior. For example, if you want a youth to take a shower every day (the youth has not been doing this regularly), then each time the youth takes a shower, he or she should receive a positive consequence. By receiving a positive consequence each time he or she takes a shower, the youth will soon learn to take a shower every day. After a behavior is learned, an intermittent schedule of reinforcement can be used. On an intermittent schedule, reinforcers for a target behavior are delivered occasionally, not every time. Reinforcers may be provided every other time or every third time the behavior is performed, or the first time the behavior occurs each hour, or after two days or three days of school attendance, or on any other schedule based on frequency or time.

Take, for example, a situation where taking a shower is no longer a new behavior for a youth, but you still want it to continue. You should now award positive consequences occasionally (e.g. every other day, every third day, etc.). However, you still should praise the youth for showering every day (continuous schedule). This praise will reinforce your relationship with the youth and make the youth feel good about showering. It seems a little illogical, but intermittent schedules of reinforcement actually strengthen behavior even more than a continuous schedule. Intermittent schedules help to fade the consequences to a more reality-based schedule, where reinforcers are not provided each time a youngster does something well.

▶ **Shaping behavior**

Child-care staff members may sometimes find that the reinforcement they are using is not changing a specific behavior. They should look again at the principles of reinforcement and decide whether the goal behavior is too difficult or too much for the youth. The staff then should use shaping to deal with the behavior. In order to shape behaviors, the following steps are useful:

1. Clearly describe the goal behavior

2. Select a behavior that comes close to the desired behavior

3. Reinforce the approximate behavior until it occurs consistently

4. Repeat until the goal behavior is achieved

An example of shaping would be helping a youth with a short attention span to concentrate on homework for a one-hour period. The youth currently starts her homework but doesn't finish it. She may sit and fidget, doodle, or talk to herself. You should set the goal of having the youth work on her homework for one hour every night during placement. Then, clearly instruct the youth that if she can quietly do her homework for five minutes, she can earn a positive consequence. When the five minutes have passed, praise the youth and give the positive consequence, using an Effective Praise interaction if the youth has met your expectations. If the youth does not meet the requirements, she should receive a negative consequence. If the child can reach the five-minute goal at least six times, you can consider setting a longer time frame (e.g. 10 minutes) and keep expanding the time period until the youth can work continuously for one hour. If the youth fails, repeat the steps or examine the reinforcers.

▶ Response cost

Sometimes, youth behave inappropriately even though they are aware of the negative consequences for that behavior. Response cost means taking away a known positive reinforcer when a target behavior that needs to be decreased occurs. A loss of positive reinforcers does decrease behavior, and in that way it functions as a punisher. However, punishment is usually thought of as the application of some aversive stimulus. (Aversive stimuli of any kind are not part of the Boys Town Family Home Program.) Response cost is different in that it takes away something positive rather than adding something negative. Thus, a youth might get a negative consequence for an inappropriate behavior. This consequence is a response cost for the behavior.

The same conditions that affect the effectiveness of positive reinforcement also affect response cost: immediacy, choice of the reinforcer to be taken away, amount of the reinforcer withheld, and withholding the reinforcer in response to a behavior. Child-care workers need to consider these conditions to maximize the effectiveness of the consequences they use for each individual youth.

▶ Generalization

Ultimately, child-care workers want their youth to be able to use appropriate behaviors without the need for tangible reinforcers, and to use their new skills in settings outside the youth-care facility. Generalization means that skills learned under one set of antecedent conditions are used under different antecedent conditions. This principle of behavior means that each skill does not have to be taught in each new environment in order for it to be used in those new environments. Generalization can be promoted by having the youth thoroughly practice each skill, and by having the practice occur under conditions that are as similar as possible to the youth's real environments (e.g. home, school, recreation area). You can actively promote generalization by monitoring how youth are behaving in a variety of environments. This monitoring can occur through home notes, school notes, phone calls, or information from other youth. This feedback enables you to reinforce youth for generalizing appropriate behavior to a variety of settings, like school or home.

▶ Discrimination

Discrimination means that changes in the antecedent conditions produce changes in behavior. Discrimination is the opposite of generalization. Discrimination means that a behavior is performed only under certain circumstances but not under other, different circumstances. Thus, what a youth does in a gymnasium is very different from what he or she does in a church. Similarly, aggression that is appropriate in an athletic contest is not appropriate at home, and greeting skills that are used with adults are different from those used with friends. When a youth uses behaviors and skills that are appropriate to a situation, it indicates that he or she has learned that certain situations call for certain behaviors. Much of the teaching done by staff members not only is helping the youth learn new skills, but also is teaching the youth where and under what conditions certain behaviors are appropriate. Teaching youth discrimination is crucial. They must learn to identify the environmental cues that call for different sets of behavior.

Summary

Understanding the principles of behavior helps child-care workers to better understand why youth get into trouble, why they become depressed, why they have emotional outbursts, and why they lack many skills necessary for normal development. Child-care workers can see how misplaced contingencies, inconsistent consequences, and unpredictable environments could help shape a youth's inappropriate behavior. Youth with behavior problems are victims of environments that reinforced many inappropriate behaviors.

As important as it is to understand how youth might have learned to be the way they are, child-care workers cannot stop there. They must intervene and try to reverse the learning that has occurred in the 10, 12, or 14 years prior to a youth's referral to the youth-care facility. They must interrupt the automatic behavior and thoughtfully use the principles of behavior to teach the youth alternative, more appropriate behaviors. This gives the youth options. With options, the youth can stop, think, and choose the behavior they want. If child-care workers can teach their youth to think and solve problems rationally, and teach them several alternative behaviors so they have choices to make, they have done their jobs.

Model comparisons

As mentioned earlier, three of the six treatment models we are comparing have a basis in learning theory or principles of behavior. These are the Boys Town Model, the Behavioral Model, and the eclectic-based University of Oklahoma program. The other three programs — the Psychodynamic (Medical) Model, Cognitive Model, and Positive Peer Culture — are based on changing feelings and thoughts, which may lead to behavior change. The programs that use principles of behavior focus on changing behavior, which leads to a change in thoughts and feelings.

In the Psychodynamic Model, the therapist or counselor helps the child talk about his or her feelings regarding the past. The child's current behavior or current environment are not considered significant factors in changing the child's feelings. The therapist believes that he or she can begin to change those feelings only by learning how they were developed during early childhood.

The Cognitive Model would take a similar approach, although it contends that events that occurred later in the child's life may have had as much impact as his or her early life experiences. Again, this model typically does not focus on changing the child's current behavior or stimuli.

Obviously, the Behavioral Model relies entirely upon the principles of behavior. The behaviorist would consider these principles constantly throughout the treatment of the child. He or she would strongly believe that the child's inappropriate behavior is not caused by the child's feelings, but are simply skill deficits that can be changed simply by manipulating the stimuli. As the antecedent and consequences are changed, the behaviorist could shape the child's behavior to what he or she wants. Then a reinforcement schedule of the new behavior could be established so the child will maintain that behavior. As mentioned earlier, the problem with approaching the child's behavior in this manner is that the child is only passively involved and the behavior could become rote or robotic.

The Boys Town Model also is deeply rooted in the principles of behavior. This program is based on the belief that a child's inappropriate behavior is due to a skill deficit. Pairing this belief with the relationship-building aspect and the active participation of the child in the treatment process, however, makes the Boys Town Model's goal different from that of the Behavioral Model. In the Boys Town Model, the goal is to help children understand and internalize the new skills they are developing so they begin to respond to the natural reinforcers in the environment. Typically, this is when the child begins to build strong relationships and his or her thoughts and feelings begin to become more positive.

As discussed in the previous chapter, the University of Oklahoma program uses a behavioral base for its behavior management section. This section utilizes many aspects of the principles of behavior. Other aspects of the program focus on thoughts and feelings and are less specific. Having such a variety of theories interwoven in the program could make replication difficult and confusing.

A Positive Peer Culture program probably would make little use of the principles of behavior. It is doubtful that the youth who implement the child's treatment would even be aware of what these principles are. Since they would be focusing on the child's words, most of their interactions would probably center on thoughts and feelings. They would probably ask the child to analyze these situations and find out why he or she felt that way. They would view the child's behavior as a reaction to his or her feelings and thoughts rather than stimuli.

CHAPTER SIX

Overview of motivation systems

One of the key ingredients to the success of the Boys Town Family Home Program is the child-care staff's daily teaching of skills and behaviors. When youth learn alternative ways of behaving, they have more options to solve problems and a better basis on which to build relationships. However, many youth who come to treatment programs are not motivated to learn or change their behavior. Many do not respond to natural consequences of their environment. Until the youth begin to respond to these positive and negative natural social consequences, an artificial means of motivating them is necessary. That is why the Motivation Systems are part of the Boys Town Family Home Program teaching process. In many ways, the structured Motivation System is like the plaster cast physicians use to help heal a broken leg. It is very important to the healing process and its removal is a good sign that progress is being made.

The Boys Town Motivation Systems are designed so that youth earn positive consequences (usually points) for appropriate behavior and are given negative consequences for inappropriate behavior. The points youth earn can be exchanged for a variety of privileges. The Motivation System a youth is on determines which privileges he or she can purchase.

Most positive consequences (positive points) are given during Effective Praise interactions, which will be discussed in detail in Chapter 9. Negative consequences (point losses) occur during Teaching Interactions (Chapter 10).

Consequences are important to the behavior change process, but they are no more or less important than any of the other teaching components. If child-care workers rely too much on the Motivation Systems, it may hinder a youth's development by not exposing him or her to natural consequences. The child might perform only for points rather than learning to respond to social and environmental contingencies.

On the other hand, if child-care workers do not use the Motivation Systems enough, their effectiveness as teachers is reduced and the youth do not learn as quickly. It is important to remember that consequences help change behavior.

Boys Town developed its Motivation Systems to help staff members improve and expand their personal ability to motivate, discipline, and monitor youth behavior. The Motivation Systems can help, but they cannot do the real work. Motivation Systems do not teach kids; staff members teach kids! Motivation Systems do not work by themselves. Ultimately, their effectiveness depends upon the cooperation of the youth and the skills of the child-care staff. Staff members need to use the systems as a tool to complement their own skills and abilities as they teach the youth to become more competent adolescents and adults. As the youth learn more skills and learn to enjoy the natural benefits of appropriate behavior, they are faded off the Motivation Systems.

▶ Token economy

Consequences can be natural or applied. Natural consequences are the typical outcomes of a behavior without any intentional human intervention. For example, scrapes and bruises are often the natural con-

sequences of falling down on a cement sidewalk. Losing weight is the natural consequence of cutting down on calorie intake.

Applied consequences for behavior are outcomes that are deliberately arranged. In the Boys Town Family Home Program, applied consequences take the form of points or tokens that youth earn for appropriate behavior and lose for inappropriate behavior. Thus, earning tokens or points is an applied consequence for answering math problems correctly or learning to greet a visitor. As an applied consequence, tokens or points are effective only because they can be exchanged for a wide range of privileges such as snacks, TV time, free time, allowance, etc. Points and tokens become "conditioned reinforcers" because they are paired with the availability of privileges. Privileges are referred to as "back-up" reinforcers because they already have proven effective in motivating youth. If points or tokens could not be used to purchase privileges, they would not be effective as applied consequences.

Why use applied consequences like points? Why not use natural or "back-up" reinforcers or privileges directly? Because applied consequences have a number of properties that make them preferable to directly using natural consequences.

1. Applied consequences such as points resist satiation. This means that youth will continue to find them to be reinforcing over long periods of time because points represent all privileges. Repeated direct use of a privilege to reinforce a behavior could result in satiation — the youngster grows tired of the reinforcer and it loses its effectiveness.

2. Points are readily available. They are convenient to deliver any time or any place; it is not always possible to provide a privilege.

3. Because points are readily available, they can be delivered as soon as a behavior occurs. This immediacy helps to strengthen the connection, and thereby helps to increase the effectiveness and power of the consequence. This means that youth can better understand the relationship between their behavior and achieving goals or avoiding problems.

4. Because points are always available and can be delivered immediately, child-care workers can make these applied consequences very predictable. Every time the behavior occurs, consequences follow. This consistency also helps the youth learn new skills and behaviors more quickly.

5. Applied consequences such as points can be used in proportion to the difficulty of the skill being learned, and to reinforce small improvements as well as large achievements. This sensitive application helps the youth learn the new behavior and experience some immediate success for his or her efforts. Eventually the skillful use of the new behavior will be followed by positive, natural consequences.

▶ Privileges and rights

Youth should have a wide variety of privileges available to them. Depending on the system, the privileges may be freely available or the youth might have to purchase them with the points they earned. At Boys Town, the types of privileges available to youth include:

1. Basics — a group of privileges that are easy to monitor and control, such as playing basketball outside, and playing in the recreation room.

2. Snacks — includes special goodies such as candy, donuts, chips, cookies, etc. Healthy snacks, such as fruit and vegetables, are provided to all youth and are not sold as a privilege.

3. Television — includes watching entertainment shows such as comedies, rock videos, appropriate movies, etc. News and educational programs are available to all youngsters and are not sold as a privilege.

4. Telephone — includes limited calls to friends, etc. Calls to parents, guardians, a priest, a minister, or an attorney are available to each youngster and are not sold as a privilege.

5. Outings — includes outside activities when the youth is accompanied by a legal guardian or relatives who have been approved by the legal guardian. A variety of educational and recreational activities under the direct supervision of a staff member are available to all youth each day and are not sold as a privilege.

6. Free time — this privilege may include leaving the grounds, without the direct supervision of a staff member, for a short time in the evening to go to a movie or to go skating. Youth also can have approved friends visit.

There also are privileges that are available once in a while or when special circumstances arise. Access to these privileges is tailored to a youth's individual needs and prices are negotiable, depending on individual circumstances. They are available to any youth on any Motivation System. It should be pointed out that these individualized privileges are not always sold. If they are important to the development and maintenance of the relationship between a youth and his or her caregivers, they can be offered without any point cost. Relationship variables are never bought or sold in any Boys Town program.

Points have value for the youth only if they can be exchanged for something the youth want. In the Boys Town Family Home Program, points are like money. Youth earn points and spend them on things they want. Privileges are the real reinforcers for the youth; points are the medium of exchange. Having a list of available privileges helps assure that only privileges can be earned or lost and not basic rights. Rights should never be restricted nor should they ever be earned or lost through a Motivation System. (See Chapter 13, "Youth Rights.")

▶ Keys to effective Motivation Systems

To have Motivation Systems that work to the benefit of each youth, child-care workers need to pay careful attention to how they use them. The following guidelines should be considered:

1. Privileges should be made contingent on behavior. Staff members need to be sure that the youth are earning all their privileges through the Motivation Systems. If youth can obtain privileges without paying for them, the

Motivation Systems become less effective because points are no longer the only way to get privileges.

2. Teaching and privileges should be individualized. Staff members must identify those activities and events that are important to each youth. These are the things that a youngster will work for and spend points on. These are the things that will motivate a youth to learn new behavior. As staff members learn more about a youth, this knowledge can help them tailor their teaching to best help the youth.

3. The Motivation Systems should be used with the Teaching Interaction. Motivation Systems alone do not help youngsters learn new ways of behaving. They work best when used with Teaching Interactions to help the youth learn new behaviors. Teaching is the critical element; Motivation Systems only help the learning process along.

4. Each youth should be taught the purpose and mechanics of the Motivation Systems. Staff members need to make sure that each youth understands how privileges are earned or lost, how to record the consequences, how to exchange points or tokens for privileges, and why the Motivation Systems are used. The explanations by the staff will help each youth learn the basic connections between behavior, points/tokens, and privileges.

5. Staff members should use the principles of behavior. They should give consequences (points) in response to behavior, provide them immediately, and have the size of the point/token gain or loss fit the behavior. They should not expect one-trial learning. It is unrealistic to expect a youth to learn a new skill the first

time it is taught. The use of these principles will help reinforce and strengthen appropriate behavior, weaken inappropriate behavior, and hasten the progress of each youth.

With respect to the size of a point/token reward or loss, staff members should keep in mind the idea of "least-restrictive alternative." This idea came out of court cases that involved residential treatment programs. The idea is that treatment providers should not intervene any more than necessary to accomplish a treatment purpose. Thus, point/token rewards or losses should be just large enough to change behavior.

Another idea related to the principles of behavior is shaping. (See Chapter 5.) Shaping means reinforcing approximations to desired behavior. If child-care workers want to teach a youth good conversation skills, they might heavily reinforce ten seconds of appropriate eye contact and two reasonable questions even though the other parts of the attempt at a conversation were not appropriate. It's a start, an approximation to a full set of competent conversation skills. Reinforcing any approximations to appropriate behavior helps shape the youth's skills toward greater competence in life.

6. Does the youth ever lose his or her privileges? If child-care workers always bail the youth out so they don't feel the response cost of going without their privileges after a "poor" day, the youth will quickly learn that they don't have to control their behavior because someone will see to it that they earn their privileges anyway.

7. Child-care workers should control the systems to help achieve desired results. The Boys Town Family Home Program represents an organized and systematic approach to help solve the problems of youth. The procedures are there to be helpful and, for most youth, most of the time, they work well. But, child-care workers need to be in control of those procedures and not feel limited to just those procedures. Unique problems or persistent problems call for unique solutions. Child-care workers are encouraged to use the principles of behavior and contact their supervisor to modify the system to help solve unique problems.

8. Finally, child-care workers need to focus on using positive reinforcement. Catching youth being good and reinforcing their appropriate behaviors helps build positive relationships and helps to keep the focus on developing appropriate behavior. When caregivers fail to do this, there can be too much emphasis on the negatives and inappropriate behavior. It is up to the child-care workers; they must control the systems and produce a positive and effective program where kids are learning and are happy.

▶ Mechanics of the empowerment card

So far in this chapter, we've discussed the Boys Town Motivation Systems and how youth earn or lose points for their behaviors. Now it is time to discuss how youth and staff members keep track of those points and the interactions in which they are given.

Youth in Boys Town programs record the points they earn or lose each day on an empowerment card. Figure 1 shows the two sides of an empowerment card.

The front of the card is divided into seven areas or columns:

1. Upper left-hand corner — spaces for the youth's name and current Motivation System.

2. Upper right-hand corner — the code that is used to identify the general types of behavior for which youth can earn or lose points, and target skills.

F-T stands for Family-Teachers, the married couple that cares for youth in a Boys Town Family Home. Each home also has an Assistant Family-Teacher (AFT), who helps the Family-Teachers with the youth.

Skill — skills are divided into three categories:

♦ Social behaviors involve interactions with other people (following instructions, positive statements, problem-solving). These behaviors are designated by a "1."

♦ Independent-living behaviors involve skills that youth must learn to be self-sufficient (cleaning, cooking, self-care, etc.). These behaviors are designated by a "2."

♦ Academic behaviors involve interactions with teachers, or school-related materials or situations (studying, homework, class participation). These behaviors are designated by a "3."

Whenever a youth earns or loses points, the number that corresponds to the type of behavior involved is written in the column labeled "SK." For many youth, a typical distribution of points earned might be about 40 to 50 percent for social behavior, 20 to 30 percent for academic behavior, and 20 to 30 percent for independent-living behavior.

3. Target — target skills are areas that will receive special emphasis when a staff member teaches a youth. The target skills are recorded in the specified area on the back of the empowerment card. The numbers that correspond with each target skill are written in the "TS" column (Target Skill) when points are earned or lost for those skills.

4. Positive points — the number of points earned is recorded in this column. Point values can vary from 100 to several thousand.

5. Curriculum skill — the name of the skill that is being taught is written in this column. Chapter 2, "Teaching Social Skills," lists many of the skills that are part of the Boys Town curriculum (e.g. listening to others, following instructions, disagreeing appropriately, asking permission, acknowledgments, asking for clarification, etc.).

6. Specific behavior — the specific behavior or event that earned a consequence is noted in this column. When appropriate behavior occurs, a youth earns positive points. Points are lost when an inappropriate behavior occurs or when an appropriate behavior is not used. In any case, you should use specific descriptions of behaviors to help the youth understand the appropriate and inappropriate behaviors that apply to each curriculum skill. For example, the curriculum skill of "listening to others" is made up of specific behaviors such as "look at the person, sit or stand quietly, think about what is being said, give an

Figure 1

Name: _____

System: ❏ Daily ❏ Sub-System _____
  ❏ Weekly ❏ Other _____

	0	1	2	3	4
F-T	MGR	MFT	FFT	AFT	
SKILL		SOCIAL	INDEPDT	ACADEMIC	
TARGET	NONE				
+ / -	-	+	PC		

Pos. Points	Curriculum Skill	Specific Behavior	Neg. Points	FT	SK	TS	+/-	FT
			Front					
	Total Positives (This Side)	Total Negatives (This Side)						

Date _____ Day _____
Name _____
Privileges Earned: ❏ Yes ❏ No
❏ Basics ❏ Snacks ❏ TV ❏ Phone ❏ Free Time ❏ Other

TARGET SKILLS
1 _____ 3 _____
2 _____ 4 _____

Pos. Points	Curriculum Skill	Specific Behavior	Neg. Points	FT	SK	TS	+/-	FT
			Back					
	TOTAL POSITIVES (This Side)	TOTAL NEGATIVES (This Side)		TAUGHT TODAY				
	TOTAL POSITIVES (Front)	TOTAL NEGATIVES (Front)		❏ MFT				
	TOTAL MADE	TOTAL LOST		❏ FFT				
	(Minus) TOTAL LOST			❏ AFT				
	POINT DIFFERENCE THIS CARD	System Standing _____						

acknowledgment, and ask for clarification (if needed)." Other specific behaviors such as arguing, yelling, cursing, or glaring would be inappropriate and would result in point losses.

7. Negative points — the number of points lost is recorded in this column.

8. FT — (the column at the far right side of the card) the Family-Teacher or child-care worker puts his or her initials in this column to verify the point transaction. ("FT" stands for Family-Teacher. Again, this card also is used in the Boys Town residential programs.)

The back of the card contains the following:

1. Name — the youth's name is written again to identify the card.

2. Privileges earned — check "Yes" or "No" to indicate whether the youth earned privileges. Check the boxes next to the privileges that were earned.

3. Day of week/Date — checking the appropriate day and entering the date identifies the card and helps in filing and retrieving information.

4. System standing — this total refers to the number of points a youngster needs to complete a particular Motivation System.

5. Totals — these areas on the back of the empowerment card help to calculate the Total Made, Total Lost, and the Point Difference This Card. The Point Difference is the critical calculation that determines the points available to purchase privileges.

6. Target skills — curriculum skills that need special attention each day are written in these spaces. You or the youngster also can use the space to note any special events or circumstances that might be in effect (e.g. "dentist appointment at 4 p.m.")

7. Taught today — in this box, the Family-Teachers (or child-care worker) check off who taught the youth that day. This provides information for future treatment and teaching strategies. MFT stands for "Male Family-Teacher," FFT is for "Female Family-Teacher," and AFT is for "Assistant Family-Teacher."

▶ Using an empowerment card

Usually, each youngster carries a empowerment card and a pencil or pen which allows point transactions to occur easily and quickly. However, some caregivers prefer to keep empowerment cards in folders or pockets on a bulletin board between point interactions. This keeps the cards neater and more legible, and keeps them in one place so caregivers can quickly review each youngster's progress any time.

When a point transaction occurs, the youngster writes down the point value, the curriculum skill, and the specific behavior on the card. The caregiver provides the information, but the youngster must write it on the card. This helps keep the youth's attention on how many points he or she has earned or lost, and the behavior that resulted in a point consequence. It also helps a youngster learn handwriting, spelling, and how to write larger numbers. Younger children or youngsters who have not done well in school often need more help with letters and numbers, and with spelling even simple words. For these youth, each point transaction takes on extra educational dimensions.

A youngster starts a new card each day during a total-up conference, when points that were earned or lost are added up. After filling in his or her name, and the date, day of week, and system, the youth records the privileges he or she has earned for the next day and completes the System Standing space (if needed). A caregiver reviews the card and suggests changes or approves the information before the youngster leaves the total-up conference. Also during the total-up conference, the caregiver should review the completed card, praise progress toward treatment goals, set goals for the next day, calculate the new System Standing, and offer a lot of praise and encouragement to each youngster. After the total-up conference, the youth can immediately begin earning or losing points.

▶ Summary

The Motivation Systems and the empowerment card are important tools in helping youth to learn new social skills. Using a token economy to reinforce appropriate behavior provides youth with an incentive to improve their behavior. Making these tools a natural part of your teaching will help you be more effective in your interactions with youth. Your knowledge also will enable you to explain to youth how to fill out their cards themselves, another step toward helping them learn responsibility and independence.

▶ Model comparisons

Since motivation systems are typically used to help motivate a child to change his or her behavior in some way, it is doubtful that this approach would be used in the Psychodynamic (Medical) Model. It is easy to have a child earn or lose something based on his or her behavior because behavior is something that can be seen and measured. It would be virtually impossible to do this with a child's feelings or thoughts because they can't be seen, and it would be difficult to know precisely what was being reinforced. Therapists can assume what a child is thinking or feeling based on what the child tells them, but they can't know for sure since they can't see the thoughts or feelings. Also, since using a motivation system changes the stimuli (consequence), the Psychodynamic therapist probably would not feel this was relevant to treatment. The Psychodynamic therapist believes that the key to the child's problem lies in analyzing events that occurred very early in the child's life, instead of focusing on what is affecting his or her immediate behavior.

Cognitive therapists also focus on a child's thoughts and feelings. Although they might do this in a more active manner, using objects, the emphasis would not be on the child's current behavior, or what is motivating it. Therefore, it is unlikely that they would use a motivation system with the child.

Behavioral therapists, on the other hand, would be very likely to use some form of motivation for the child, although it would not necessarily be a formal type of system. Their whole philosophy is based on the premise that events that occur immediately after a behavior can either increase or decrease the behavior. Consequently, they would find the use of some form of motivation essential if they were trying to increase a positive behavior in a child. They may attempt to do this by altering something in the environment, changing the social reinforcers the child receives, or using some form of artificial reinforcement, such as a motivation system.

Since the Boys Town Model calls for the child to be actively involved in the treatment process, and contends that events that follow a child's behavior affect the behavior, a positive, rewarding Motivation System is part of the treatment program. The main purpose of this system is to provide reinforcers for the child's positive behavior with the hope of increasing it. If the child is spending more time engaging in positive behaviors, he or she should be spending less time engaging in inappropriate ones.

As mentioned in the chapter on principles of behavior, negative events that immediately follow a behavior can decrease the behavior. Therefore, caregivers are encouraged to provide consequences for inappropriate behavior. This balance of providing reinforcement for appropriate behavior and consequences for inappropriate behavior helps the child to quickly understand the importance of engaging in socially appropriate behavior. This helps the child begin to build relationships faster with the caregivers and others.

In the behavior management section of the eclectic-based University of Oklahoma program, caregivers are encouraged to use reinforcers with children. The emphasis is on the importance of reinforcing the child for positive behavior so the behavior will increase. Caregivers are given the option of doing this with social reinforcers, rewards, or token economies. No specific motivation systems are provided, so the caregiver must decide what type of reinforcement is going to be used and how it will be structured. This lack of specificity could make it difficult to recognize this program across settings, since caregivers can structure their programs to their own standards. This would make it difficult to train others in the program or provide consultation, and would make it very difficult to evaluate how well the program is being carried out.

Positive Peer Culture programs probably would not use any type of motivation system. Since most of these programs use some form of group therapy in their treatment, they would not be concerned with controlling the reinforcers or consequences that would immediately follow a child's behavior. As mentioned earlier, the group focuses on encouraging youth to share their thoughts and feelings while their peers respond to them. Since most of the discussion involves rethinking past events, there is little concern for the child's current behavior, unless it is somehow affecting the group itself.

CHAPTER SEVEN

Recognizing and describing behavior

The problems that lead to placement in a youth-care facility are varied but almost always result in tremendous youth skill deficits. These skill deficits can take many behavioral forms (i.e. school truancy, stealing, not following parental rules, or fighting).

But there is a positive side to this. Because these behaviors have been learned, and many of them inappropriately reinforced over a long period of time, they also can be changed, eliminated, or replaced with more socially appropriate behavior. Certainly, dramatic changes in a youth's behavior cannot be expected to occur overnight. Rather, the rate of change will vary from youth to youth based on many factors related to the experiences of each youth. As a child-care worker, you play a significant role in helping the youth learn "new" appropriate ways of responding through teaching and modeling, communicating expectations and setting clear limits, the systematic and consistent use of appropriate consequences (both positive and negative), and by fostering positive, supportive relationships.

To bring about these behavior changes, child-care workers must have a model that helps them recognize and describe behavior. This section presents ways to specifically recognize and describe behavior, and explains how to use these abilities to focus on skills during teaching procedures (i.e. Effective Praise, Corrective Teaching, Preventive Teaching, and Intensive Teaching®).

▶ The ABC Model

Human behavior is often complex, confusing, and difficult to understand.

Although one could guess why a youth behaves a certain way, it could be harmful to jump to conclusions or assumptions about that youth without having reliable information. In order to gather reliable information, child-care workers must use a systematic means of analyzing behavior.

The ABC Model provides a system for observing and describing what people do, making reasonable assumptions about why they do it, and developing strategies to maintain positive behaviors and change negative behaviors. It is based on the idea that we learn most of our behavior.

Behavior does not occur in a vacuum. Events that occur in the environment before and after a behavior can have a major impact on that behavior. Thus, it is important to understand all the circumstances surrounding a behavior if it is to be fully understood. The ABC Model comprises these elements:

A = Antecedents — the events or conditions present in the environment before a behavior occurs.

B = Behavior — what is done or said by a person.

C = Consequences — the results, outcomes, or effects of a behavior.

Questions that can be used to assess a particular behavior based on the ABC Model are listed here. These questions are pertinent when you are assessing a behavior you directly observed, or acquiring information about an indirect observation (e.g. getting facts from a schoolteacher about a youth behavior problem).

The ABC Model: Analysis questions

Antecedent

What were the circumstances surrounding the behavior?

With whom did the behavior occur (child-care worker, parent, friend, teacher)?

What activity was the youth involved in (watching TV, playing a game, talking on the phone, requesting permission)?

When did the behavior occur (morning, afternoon, evening, weekend, school night)?

Where did the behavior occur (residential facility, school, friend's house, bedroom)?

Behavior

What is the youth doing?

What are the youth's body movements (walking around, clenching fists, hugging)?

What are the youth's facial expressions (smiling, frowning, batting eyes, rolling eyes, eye contact)?

How is the youth expressing himself or herself verbally (loud, soft, swearing, laughing, crying)?

How intense is the behavior?

How long does it last? How often does it happen?

Consequence

What is the outcome of the behavior?

What happened during or after the behavior?

Was the behavior reinforced so it may occur again?

Was a corrective consequence or punishment used to decrease the behavior?

What was the response of others (walked away, argued, laughed)?

If the youth was doing some work, was the work completed?

Antecedents

When analyzing a behavior, it helps to know what happened just before the behavior that might have helped "trigger" or "signal" it — the "A" or Antecedent of the ABC Model. You should pay particular attention to the four "W's" (i.e. who, when, where, and what) to determine the antecedents. The four "W's" can work in combination or alone to set the stage for particular behaviors to occur. Furthermore, it is important that you become familiar with the youth's history to get a feeling for the previous learning that has occurred. This learning history also plays a role in the antecedents of current behavior.

While the antecedents for a behavior may be complex, it is often a more simple stimulus (or set of stimuli) that immediately precedes a behavior: A telephone ring immediately precedes someone answering the phone; a smiling face and an extended hand set the occasion for a handshake; a red light at an intersection precedes stepping on the brake in the car; and a mild argument between two youth immediately precedes a child-care

worker's behavior of intervening and teaching more appropriate behavior.

The Four "W's"

Who — with whom does the behavior occur or who is present when the behavior occurs?

When — time of day the behavior occurs (before bed, after school, during dinner, etc.).

Where — in what location does the behavior usually occur (i.e. classroom, in the bedroom, dining room, etc.)?

What — what activity is the youth engaged in (i.e. watching TV, playing with friends, walking to class, etc.)?

Behavior

While Behavior, the "B" of the ABC Model, is the second component, it is necessary for you to focus on this component first in order to understand the other two. You must determine what the behavior is before the relevant antecedents and consequences can be known.

What is behavior? Behavior is defined as anything a person does or says that can be directly or indirectly observed and measured. Behavior can be either overt or covert (Spiegler, 1983). Overt behavior refers to actions that can be directly observed by other people. Examples include eating, walking, talking, smiling, etc. Many other behaviors cannot be directly observed by other people. Such private or covert behaviors such as thoughts and feelings are known to others only indirectly and always in terms of some overt behavior. (See Figure 1.) In fact, we frequently learn about others' covert behaviors when they tell us about such behavior.

Overt behavior is any observable action or response by an individual, including:

◆ Body Movements

◆ Facial Movements or Expressions

◆ Verbal Responses

In the Boys Town Family Home Program, overt behaviors are emphasized within the ABC Model. This is because overt behaviors (Figure 1) are directly observable and can be more easily identified and targeted for change.

Consequences

The third component of the ABC Model is the "C" for Consequence. The events in the environment that follow a behavior can be pleasant, unpleasant, or neutral. That is, events or consequences that follow a behavior can be classified as reinforcing, nonreinforcing, or having no effect. Reinforcing events that follow a behavior increase the chances that the same behavior will occur again in the future. Nonreinforcing events decrease the likelihood that the behavior will occur again. Thus, knowing what happens right after a behavior occurs not only helps child-care workers analyze the behavior, but also helps them predict the future course of the behavior. For example,

answering the telephone can result in a reinforcing event like talking to a friend; a handshake can lead to a reinforcing social interaction; stopping at a red light can lead to a reinforcing event like avoiding a traffic ticket or a collision; and, teaching appropriate ways to disagree can result in more reinforcing discussions. In each of these examples, the behavior results in a pleasant consequence and, in each case, the behavior is more likely to occur again under those same antecedent conditions.

The effect of consequences on behavior

1. Behavior can be positively changed, or occur with more frequency or more intensity.

2. Behavior can be decreased, or occur less often or with less intensity.

3. New behaviors can be learned and behaviors improved.

4. Behavior can be changed so that it occurs at a different time or place.

▶ Using the ABC Model to effectively teach skills

Understanding the ABC Model will help clarify why a behavior is occurring. More importantly, it also helps child-care workers change behavior by providing a way for them to recognize and describe behavior (i.e. the ABC analysis questions). Youth are placed in residential care facilities because

Figure 1

How is covert behavior inferred?

Covert behavior	Overt behavior anchors
Silent Reading	Looking at a page of a book (for a reasonable time) Eyes moving across lines of page Lip movements while looking at page Turning pages (at reasonable time intervals)
Worrying	Pacing Saying you are worried Biting fingernails Sweating Tensing muscles Chain smoking
Feeling Happy	Smiling Laughing Saying you are happy Telling jokes Playing
Listening (to a speaker)	Looking directly at the speaker Taking notes on what the speaker is saying Verbally disagreeing with the speaker Asking the speaker questions Telling others what the speaker had to say

Adapted from **Contemporary Behavioral Therapy** (1983), by Michael Spiegler, (p. 44). Palo Alto, CA: Mayfield Publishing Company. Copyright 1983 by Mayfield Publishing Company.

they have problems that exclude them from family, friends, school, and their community. They come to residential care facilities to change their behavior and return to their homes. Using the ABC Model helps child-care workers promote change in positive, effective, and efficient ways.

How do child-care workers help change behavior? They help change behavior by changing the antecedents, the behavior, or the consequences, or all three.

Antecedents often can be changed. For example, if an adult yells at a youth when giving an instruction, the youth may respond with verbal aggression. If the adult gives the instruction in a pleasant tone of voice, the youth is less likely to respond aggressively.

New behaviors can be taught to youth and youth can be taught to not use inappropriate behaviors. For instance, a youth with "authority problems" can be taught new skills, such as how to follow instructions, how to accept criticism, or how to disagree appropriately. Similarly, a youth can be taught to not use inappropriate behaviors like speaking in a loud, threatening voice or making sarcastic statements that hurt relationships with authority figures. By changing a youth's behavior, the consequences often will change naturally. Using these skills will likely result in more pleasant interactions with adults.

Consequences also can be changed. Points can be given for each correct answer on a worksheet; points can be taken away for disruptive outbursts. Pleasant comments and comforting physical contact may follow coop-erative social behavior; frowns and a serious voice tone can follow a mild argument. By changing the consequences of behavior, a child-care worker can change the behavior itself.

▶ Benefits of observing and describing skills

Being able to observe and describe skills helps child-care workers teach behaviors more effectively. Observing and describing behavior allows child-care workers to make the youth aware of specific appropriate and inappropriate behavior. Vague or general descriptions, such as, "You need to change your attitude," or "You have really been cooperative," do not help the youth learn exactly what behaviors need to be avoided or should occur in the future. Vague, judgmental descriptions also can lead the youth to argue (e.g. "I do not have a bad attitude!", "I do cooperate!"). Some examples of vague descriptions made more specific are listed here.

Vague descriptions made specific

VAGUE Aggressive Behaviors
SPECIFIC Shaking fists, raising voice, hitting, kicking, pointing finger in face

VAGUE Temper Tantrums
SPECIFIC Crying, lying on the floor, kicking and pounding fists, throwing toys

VAGUE Good Grooming
SPECIFIC Clean, hair combed, bathed, clothes pressed, fingernails clean

VAGUE Being Home On Time
SPECIFIC Be home at 10 p.m.

VAGUE Flirting
SPECIFIC Giggling, batting eyes, looking out of corner of eye, touching, staring

VAGUE Clean Your Room
SPECIFIC Make your bed, pick everything up off the floor, put all dirty clothes in the hamper, dust off furniture, vacuum carpet, etc.

VAGUE Immature
SPECIFIC Even though she's 16, she likes to watch Saturday morning cartoons, plays with Barbies, sticks her tongue out at staff members when angry

Clear behavioral descriptions further enhance teaching effectiveness by helping youth understand what is expected. When expectations are clearly communicated, the youth is more likely to successfully learn skills. Success for the youth means that you can use your time more effectively and help the youth learn more skills.

Your relationships with the youth are enhanced by skillfully observing and describing behavior. The use of specific, objective, and behavioral descriptions helps you avoid judgmental terms (e.g. wrong, bad, stupid, terrible, etc.) that can damage a youth's self-esteem or trigger an emotional reaction. When behavioral descriptions are clear, without being judgmental, youth are more likely to view you as concerned, pleasant, and fair, and are more likely to be receptive to teaching. In fact, research has shown that

youth prefer being told exactly how and what to do, and particularly rate specific, positive feedback as important (Willner, Braukmann, Kirigin, Fixsen, Phillips, & Wolf, 1977).

▶ Building skills

Child-care workers need to use their ability to observe and describe behavior to the best benefit of the youth. This means that behaviors that are observed and described are taught in the context of skills. A skill is a set of related behaviors. When the related behaviors are appropriately used together, the youth can successfully and comfortably interact with his or her environment.

There are many discrete behaviors (e.g. looking at someone, saying "Thank you," asking a question, etc.) that you will observe and then describe to the youth. These behaviors can be combined in different ways to produce the skills that are appropriate for a situation (e.g. greeting a visitor or guest, accepting a compliment, following instructions, etc.). Just as nails are used in building many different structures, behaviors such as looking at a person are used in a variety of skills.

Labeling skills and breaking them down into specific behaviors within the context of teaching has many advantages for you and your youth. It makes the teaching process more efficient and more meaningful for the youth. The process is more efficient because several behaviors can be taught at the same time. The outcome is more meaningful and valuable to the youth because it is easier for them to generalize the new skill to other settings or antecedent conditions. After all, an important goal of teaching new ways of behaving is to not only have the youth learn something new, but also to have them know when and where the new behaviors should be used (i.e. teaching discrimination).

Although most of the teaching in Boys Town programs is focused on skills, there are occasions when the focus may, or even should be, on a behavior. Sometimes a youth will be having difficulty with an important skill component behavior such as eye contact or verbally answering requests. The behavior may be an important part of a number of skills. In such cases, you may need to focus on that behavior and later integrate the behavior into the context of skills.

Labeling skills and specifically describing behavior are most important in the first four steps of the Teaching Interaction, the nine-step process used for teaching new skills. (The Teaching Interaction will be discussed in detail in Chapter 10.) Those four steps are: 1) Initial Praise, Empathy, or Affection; 2) Description/Demonstration of Inappropriate Behavior; 3) Consequences, and 4) Description/Demonstration of Appropriate Behavior. Labeling and describing also are important when providing feedback after a youth practices a skill.

The following example is provided to help new child-care workers understand how descriptions of behavior and skill labeling fit into these four steps.

Skill labeling and behavioral description

Situation: Chris is a fairly new youth and is watching TV. A child-care worker asks Chris to get ready for bed. Chris sighs and doesn't look at the person but gets up to walk to his room. The use of the first four Teaching Interaction steps might sound something like this:

1. Initial praise, empathy, or affection

Child-care worker: "Chris, thanks for getting right up to get ready for bed. I know it's hard to follow instructions sometimes, especially when you're enjoying watching TV."

Explanation — Specific, descriptive praise was given for "getting right up." The general skill was identified in the context of the empathy statement, "I know it's hard to follow instructions...." Whenever possible, the initial praise should be related to behaviors that are part of the skill to be praised or taught.

2. Description/demonstration of inappropriate behavior

Child-care worker: "When I gave you that instruction, you sighed and didn't look at me or say anything to let me know you heard or that you were going to get ready for bed."

Explanation — The skill label "instruction" is repeated and the description includes not only the inappropriate behavior of sighing but the absence of behaviors that would have been appropriate (e.g. "You didn't look at me or say anything...."). Also note that the child-care worker avoids vague and judgmental descriptions such as, "You weren't very cooperative..." or "You didn't seem too happy when I asked you to...."

3. Consequences

Child-care worker: "So please take out your empowerment card and give yourself 1,000 negative points for not following instructions. You'll have a chance to earn some of the points back by practicing how to follow instructions."

Explanation — The use of the consequence provides an opportunity to clearly and concisely label the skill that is the focus of the interaction and to indicate that practicing the skill will enable the youth to earn back some of the points. Note: You should be sure to use phrases like "Give yourself...," or "You've earned...," when delivering consequences rather than, "I'm taking away...," or "I'm going to give you...." The former phrasing helps the youth understand that he, not the child-care worker, owns the behavior and is responsible for the consequences. Negative consequences help decrease the probability that problem behavior will occur in the future.

4. Description/demonstration of appropriate behavior

Child-care worker: "Chris, let's talk about following instructions. Whenever anyone gives you an instruction, whether it's a teacher, your parents, or your employer, there are several things you should do. You should look at the person and answer them by saying 'Okay' or 'Sure,' or something to let the person know you're listening and will follow through. Do the task and then check back with the person when you're done."

Explanation — The child-care worker helps the youth generalize the skill to other situations by explaining the antecedent condition, "Whenever anyone gives you an instruction...." Then he or she provides a clear, step-by-step behavioral description to help the youth learn the skill. During the interaction, the child-care worker should pause frequently to ask the youth if he understands, has any questions, etc.

▶ Summary

In summary, the ability to observe and describe behaviors is a key element in effective teaching. You can be a pleasant, effective teacher by carefully observing and describing behavior using the ABC Model, by labeling skills and describing the behaviors related to them, and by skillfully integrating these techniques into the components of the Teaching Interaction.

Understanding the reasons for and results of a youth's behavior can help child-care workers develop effective responses when certain behaviors occur. Recognizing when a problem situation is about to occur can help child-care workers prevent behaviors that might otherwise damage relationships or lead to more serious problems. Clear specific descriptions of appropriate and inappropriate behaviors convey expectations to youth and enhance the teaching of social skills.

▶ Model comparisons

Recognizing and describing behavior is a key to successfully carrying out programs that are based on the principles of behavior. To change a behavior, the person first must recognize the behavior, then be able to describe the behavior very specifically so it can be broken down into the steps involved. Obviously, programs that lean more toward discussing thoughts and feelings would not have a strong need to recognize and describe behavior.

This is the case with the Psychodynamic (Medical) Model. Since the therapist is not focusing on the child's current behavior problems, it would be unlikely that he or she would need to describe behavior during the therapy. Even in discussing past events with the child, the therapist would stress the importance of having the child recall his or her thoughts and feelings during those events rather than what behaviors occurred.

The same would be true for the Cognitive Therapy Model. During treatment, the therapist would probably have the child use objects to reenact events in his or her life. The emphasis would be on having the child recall how he or she felt during these events, rather than the child's behavior during this time.

On the other hand, a therapist using the Behavioral Model definitely needs to be able to recognize and describe behavior. Since the total focus of therapy is identifying the antecedents and consequences to a child's behavior, the therapist must be able to notice small details of behavior to know how to facilitate change. The therapist typically would spend a great deal of time observing the child's behavior, and make treatment decisions based on those observations.

A child-care worker in the Boys Town program needs to learn how to recognize and describe behavior, as well. Since the Boys Town Motivation Systems will be used to reinforce or correct a child's behavior, the caregiver must be able to recognize the behavior accurately and use the Motivation Systems accordingly. Since the child is actively involved in the treatment, it also is important that the caregiver can specifically describe the behavior to the child. If the behavior is described specifically, the child learns what needs to be changed and how to go about it. This helps the children experience success since they have a clear idea of exactly what they need to do.

A child-care worker in the eclectic-based University of Oklahoma program needs some understanding of recognizing and describing behavior to successfully implement the program. Although this section of the model is based on behavioral principles, workers are not taught how to recognize a child's behavior or how to break it down into specific steps for the child. Since most people tend to focus on subjective feelings about the child (e.g. "You have a bad attitude" or "You're really making me mad"), it would be difficult to describe behavior objectively without some guidance in how to do it. If the worker cannot specifically describe the child's behavior, the child's chances of learning a new behavior are reduced.

In a Positive Peer Culture program, there typically is little focus on the child's behavior unless it is affecting the group. Since the group's focus is the discussion of feelings and thoughts, group members probably would not find it necessary to recognize or describe behavior.

CHAPTER EIGHT

Rationales

A rationale, or reason, is a statement that explains to a youth the relationship between his or her behavior and the consequences or outcomes of the behavior. For example, the rationale for practicing a sport is that the players probably will do better in a game. The rationale for being on time at work is that an employer might use that as one reason to give an employee a raise.

Research in the Boys Town Family Home Program suggests that rationales are most effective when they indicate a personal benefit for the youth. For example, you could tell a youth that the reason he or she should study hard is to improve his or her grades. But if the youth is much more interested in sports than school, a more personally beneficial rationale would be that studying hard can lead to good grades, allowing the youth to go out for football. Or, you might tell a youth that the reason she should follow instructions is to save time so she can talk to friends on the telephone. This rationale is more personally beneficial than telling a youth to follow instructions so that the home or program runs more smoothly.

As you teach, it is important to point out the personal benefits of the appropriate behavior whenever possible. Certainly, there will be times when you will find it necessary to provide a rationale that points out the possible negative outcomes of a youth's behavior (e.g. when a youth destroys property). However, if negative rationales are used too often, they may begin to sound like warnings or threats (e.g. "John, if you don't follow instructions you are going to get into more trouble."). It is more effective to use positive rationales to encourage appropriate behavior.

Giving a youth a reason for doing something can set the stage for a long discussion or even an argument about the validity of the rationale. You can avoid this kind of unproductive discussion by explaining to the youth that he or she is not expected to agree with the rationale. The youth should, however, be asked if he or she understands what was said (i.e. Was the rationale stated clearly enough that the youth could repeat it?). A rationale should never be used as coercive logic for why a youth should perform a behavior. Rather, it should indicate to the youth why you believe the new behavior is important enough to take the time and energy to teach it.

▶ Importance of rationales

Rationales are important for teaching youth the relationship between their behavior and what happens to them. Many youth do not fully understand the relationship between their behavior and subsequent events. For example, D.S. Eitzen (1974) conducted a survey of the attitudes of predelinquent and delinquent adolescents and found that they did not understand that their behavior determines what happens to them. Often, youth see themselves as "victims of fate." For example, if Fred gets a "D" in English, he may blame the teacher for assigning the grade instead of looking at his failure to turn in homework as the real reason for the grade.

The relationships between these events must be carefully taught. By using rationales, you help youth learn the important relationship between their behavior and the various consequences that might result.

Examples of rationales

"By getting a chore done correctly the first time, you won't have to do it over again and you'll have more time for yourself."

"When you respect others' space by standing an arm's length away from them, they will want to be around you more and will be more likely to start conversations with you."

"If you can accept 'No' for an answer appropriately, you are more likely to get a 'Yes' answer later on."

"When you share your stereo with someone, that person will be more likely to share something he or she has with you."

"If you ask for help when you don't know how to do something, you are more likely to get the job done right and won't have to redo it later."

▶ Benefits of rationales

The most important benefit of using rationales is the one discussed earlier in this chapter: Rationales help teach youth the relationships between their behavior and the various consequences that result. Another benefit of using rationales is that it aids in building positive relationships with youth. Pikas (1961) found that youth prefer parents whose disciplinary requests are accompanied by rationales and explanations. For example, "You can't watch television right now because your homework is not finished" contains a rationale and would be preferred over the statement, "You can't watch television right now."

Rationales also help with compliance. Elder (1963) found that youngsters are more likely to comply with their parents' requests if the parents provide explanations for their rules and requests. For example, a parent might say, "If you save your money from your paper route, then you can buy a new bike." That statement contains a rationale explaining why the youngster cannot have a new bicycle now and why he or she should save money. Furthermore, Elder found that when parents provided rationales for rules and requests, their children were more likely to have confidence in their own ideas and opinions. This confidence, coupled with the youth's understanding of the relationship between their behavior and consequences, can lead to better decision-making on the part of the youth.

Since rationales can be related to values, they also can help guide a youth's moral development. For example, a rationale for being honest and not stealing might include avoiding trouble and earning more freedom, and might also focus on the fact that stealing is morally wrong. Societal benefits or moral values can and should be included as rationales. However, it is best to use personally beneficial rationales when teaching new skills or behaviors. With the regular inclusion of rationales, youth come to better understand the relationship between their behavior and the subsequent consequences and actions of others in response to their behavior. This helps youth internalize the importance of their behavior and the new skills being learned, so that they become less dependent on external rewards and reinforcement.

With regard to Teaching Interactions or Corrective Teaching, Willner et al. (1977) found that youth prefer teaching procedures in which explanations accompany the teaching of alternative, more appropriate skills. They found that child-care workers who use rationales are more likely to be viewed as fair and be liked by the youth. Thus, the use of rationales seems to be important for teaching the youngsters as well as developing positive relationships between the child-care staff and youth.

▶ Components of rationales

To be effective, rationales should:

1. Point out natural consequences. Rationales should emphasize the benefits that are likely to occur if a youth engages in the appropriate behavior. For example, "If you work hard and discuss your feelings with your therapist, you'll make more progress, and be able to go home sooner."

2. Be personal to the youth. You should observe each youth to determine his or her interests, favorite activities, and likes or dislikes. Then, rationales can be specially tailored to each youth. For example, if a particular child enjoys playing computer games, you might say, "If you follow instructions and get your homework done, you'll be able to play computer games this evening." By gearing rationales to the individual interests of each youth, you increase the likelihood that a youth will accept the rationale and learn the skill being taught. For a new youth, this is not always possible until you get to know him or her better. In those situations, you can rely on a token or point system. For example, you might tell a youth, "If you learn to follow instructions, you can earn positive points." Point system rationales should be faded out systematically so the youth learn to see the natural positive or negative consequences of their behavior instead of relying on artificial consequences.

3. Be specific and brief. Usually, one good brief rationale is enough to accomplish the purposes of a teaching procedure (e.g. Effective Praise or Teaching Interaction). At times, you might think, "If I give him enough reasons for why he should do this, he will see the logic of it and have no excuse for not doing it." This approach almost always fails since the youth will probably feel he or she is being "preached at," and become angry or bored. One or possibly two brief rationales will usually keep the youth's interest and adequately explain why you want to teach this behavior.

4. Be believable and short-term. Rationales are more effective when immediate natural consequences, rather than long-term events, are emphasized. (See Number 5 for exceptions.) Thus, a rationale for following instructions without arguing might be, "You will have more free time if you promptly follow instructions instead of wasting time arguing." Pointing out this short-term, believable consequence is preferable to providing a remote consequence such as, "When you play basketball next year, the coach will be more likely to let you start if you can follow instructions." Also, rationales must be believable, which means they must be age-appropriate and personalized. For example, you might tell a nine-year-old who enjoys playing with toy cars, "If you keep your room clean you will be able to

find your cars and they will be less likely to be lost or broken." But a 17-year-old girl who is concerned about her appearance might be told, "If you keep your room neat, your clothes will look neater and cleaner, and you'll be able to find the clothes you want quickly."

5. Be varied to fit the developmental needs and maturity of the youth. In general, rationales that point out personal benefits and that are short-term and believable are preferred. This is especially true for youth who are new to a youth-care facility or are less developmentally mature. However, on occasion and as youth develop and begin to internalize the gains they have made, it also is important to use rationales that point out long-term consequences and are other-oriented and include concern for others. Long-term rationales point out more general consequences related to a youth's behavior — consequences that will occur at some point in the more distant future. It is important for youth to understand how their behavior may affect their employment, their ability to take care of themselves, and their ability to develop and maintain relationships. For example, a long-term rationale related to accepting criticism might focus on the youth's ability to get along in the future with a spouse, or to keep a job.

Similarly, you need to provide rationales that point out how a youth's behavior affects others. Such "other-oriented" rationales include sensitivity and concern for others and teach youth that their behaviors leave an impression on other people. They need to know that such impressions reflect not only on them as individuals, but also on everyone in the facility. For example, an other-oriented rationale for not teasing others might be, "Teasing others might make them feel uncomfortable or hurt their feelings." Thus, rationales can point out how the behavior of each youth affects others and how it can benefit or harm the other youth he or she lives with, and the reputation of the entire facility as well.

When to use rationales

The appropriate use of rationales in the context of various Boys Town Family Home Program components and procedures will be discussed later. (See Chapters 9, 10, and 11.) Briefly, rationales are used in the following contexts.

1. In Teaching Interactions — In a Teaching Interaction, the Rationale follows these four steps: Initial Praise, Empathy, or Affection; Description of Inappropriate Behavior; Consequences; and Description of Appropriate Behavior. Rationales used in a Teaching Interaction point out the benefits of the appropriate behavior and, when necessary, the harms of the inappropriate behavior.

2. In Preventive Teaching — Rationales are used in Preventive Teaching when new skills are taught to a youth. In Preventive Teaching, the Rationale follows Initial Praise, Empathy, or Affection; Consequences; and Description of Appropriate Behavior. These rationales point out the benefits of using the new, appropriate behavior being taught.

3. In Effective Praise — Rationales also are a part of Effective Praise, where child-care workers use Praise, Rationales, and Positive Consequences to reinforce appropriate behavior as it occurs. Effective Praise is an important method that supplements Teaching Interactions and encourages the youth to make general use of the skills being taught.

4. In daily life — In daily interactions with youth, there will be numerous informal occasions for child-care workers to provide rationales. Youth might ask your opinion, or you might offer advice or a point of view. Including rationales at every opportunity is extremely helpful!

Summary

A youth is more likely to perceive you as less arbitrary and more concerned if rationales are systematically provided. Additionally, youth are more likely to recognize the real-life consequences of their actions if they have been pointed out through a rationale, and are more likely to engage in the new behavior if they can see some way that it will benefit them.

Even though rationales are very important and have many uses, you should not think that rationales change behavior. Real changes in youth behavior result from teaching or reinforcing social skills through the use of praise, positive consequences for appropriate behavior, negative consequences for inappropriate behavior, and clear and specific descriptions of behavior, along with rationales. Rationales are a necessary component, but do not, by themselves, change behavior.

▶ Model comparisons

Rationales are reasons that show children the relationship between their behavior and the consequences or outcomes of the behavior. This can help the child understand the benefits of engaging in socially acceptable behavior.

Since the Psychodynamic (Medical) Model does not focus on behavior, the therapist probably would not use rationales in this manner. A therapist may provide reasons to the child, but these would typically be used to explain the child's feelings, not his or her behavior.

This would be true for the Cognitive Model, as well. The therapist in this model may want to explain to the child why certain things occur, but these reasons would be directed toward the feelings the child recalls, not toward current behavior.

A therapist in the Behavioral Model probably would not provide rationales. Since the child is passively involved in the therapy and the therapist is focused on changing the stimuli, the therapist would not feel that it is important to explain to the child why he or she should act a certain way. The therapist believes that shaping the behavior is enough, and that as the child begins to use this new behavior, it may lead to a change in feelings later.

In the Boys Town Model, rationales are a critical part of the treatment program. Since the program emphasizes relationship-building and actively involving the child in the treatment, providing rationales that are personally beneficial to the child helps accomplish these goals. Studies have found that children who are given rationales for their behavior are much more likely to comply with requests and rules. Also, when youth feel that staff members have a reason for asking them to engage in certain behavior, it enhances the relationship between the staff and the youth. Understanding why a behavior is important also helps the child to internalize the behavior.

Rationales are not used in the eclectic-based University of Oklahoma program. Throughout the program's behavior management section, there is a focus on behavior but it is not paired with explaining to the child why the behavior is important. This could make change slower since the child may not understand why this behavior is expected of him or her. It also could harm the staff's relationship with the child because the child may think that staff members are arbitrarily making these demands on the child's behavior.

Positive Peer Culture programs do not emphasize the use of rationales either. When a child's peers are challenging his or her thoughts and feelings, it is unlikely that they are concerned with providing rationales for why the youth should act certain ways. If this did occur, it would probably happen spontaneously, not because it is an expectation of the program.

CHAPTER NINE

Effective praise

Effective Praise is crucial to developing relationships and is very important in strengthening appropriate behavior. Effective Praise interactions enable you to sincerely and enthusiastically recognize the progress each youth is making. How the praise is given is what makes it effective in developing relationships and in reinforcing behavior. The steps of Effective Praise are:

1. Praise

2. Description of Appropriate Behavior

3. Rationale

4. Request for Acknowledgment

5. Positive Consequence

The steps of Effective Praise work together to communicate your concern for youth, as well as your approval and appreciation when the youth is behaving well and making strides to change specific inappropriate behaviors. The steps of Effective Praise are used like this:

1. Praise — Begin the interaction on a positive note by praising the youth for some appropriate behavior. The praise should be specific and genuine.

Example: "Sarah, you really did a nice job of following instructions."

2. Description of appropriate behavior —Specifically describe the youth's appropriate verbal and nonverbal behavior. This step usually begins with a description of the antecedent. Antecedents are conditions that occur prior to a behavior and help set the stage for certain responses.

Example: "When I asked you to clean your room (antecedent), you looked at me, said 'Okay,' did the task, and checked back."

3. Rationale — Provide the youth with a rationale for continuing to behave appropriately. The rationale should be youth-oriented to help the youngster internalize what she is learning and to help motivate her to change.

Example: "Sarah, by following instructions the right way, you'll have more free time to spend having fun."

4. Request for acknowledgment — Ask the youth if she understands what is being said. Requests for acknowledgment take the form of a question.

Example: "Do you understand?" or "Does that make sense to you?" or "Do you know what that means?"

5. Positive consequence — Give the youth a positive consequence for behaving appropriately. This increases the likelihood that the youth will behave appropriately in the future. Positive consequences can take the form of applied consequences such as tokens or privileges.

Example: "You have earned 2,000 positive points (tokens) for following instructions," or "For following instructions, you have earned 15 minutes of phone time (privileges)."

The following is an example of an Effective Praise interaction using all five steps.

Behavior — Following Instructions

Praise

"Mary, you really did a nice job of following that instruction."

Description of appropriate behavior

"When I asked you to make your bed, you looked at me, said 'Okay, I'll do that right away,' made your bed, and let me know you were done."

Rationale

"By following instructions right away, you don't waste your time. That way you have more free time for fun things like playing computer games."

Request for acknowledgment

"Do you understand what I mean?"

Positive consequence

"For following instructions, you have earned 2,000 positive points."

▶ Summary

There are many benefits to using praise effectively and consistently. First, it is a powerful teaching tool that is easy for child-care workers to use. Second, pointing out the specific positive behavior youth have demonstrated and complimenting them increases the chances that the behavior will occur again. As the frequency of positive behaviors increases, the incidence of negative behaviors decreases. Third, focusing on positive behaviors makes your time with the youth more pleasant and helps build positive relationships. Fourth, consistently complimenting youth for positive behaviors improves their self-concept by giving them a sense of accomplishment.

▶ Model comparisons

When using the Psychodynamic (Medical) Model, it is important for the therapist to build a relationship with the child. This is necessary for most children so that they will be willing to share their feelings with the therapist. Therefore, the therapist typically uses a great deal of empathy when talking with the child. The therapist would want the child to know that he or she accepts the child's feelings and that the child has reason to feel certain ways.

Although the therapist would be empathic with the child, it is unlikely he or she would use much praise. Most of the time, people receive praise for their behavior, not their thoughts and feelings. Since the therapist is not as concerned with the child's current behavior, he or she probably would not feel that giving praise is an important part of the treatment.

A Cognitive Model therapist would probably feel the same way. The therapist in this type of program tries to let the child know that he or she understands the child's feelings, but does not focus on the child's behavior. Since behavior is not a primary focus, the therapist probably would use little praise when interacting with the child.

This should not imply that therapists who use either of these two models do not provide a lot of praise to the children they are working with. It only means that praise is not considered part of the child's treatment.

Praise could be an important component of treatment in the Behavioral Model. Since the behaviorist is focused on changing the consequences that follow the child's behavior, he or she may use praise as a social reinforcer to increase a behavior. Praise then becomes an integral part of the treatment for shaping that particular behavior.

A strong focus of the Boys Town Model is "catching the kids being good." As mentioned earlier, if the child-care worker can increase the child's appropriate behavior, the child is less likely to engage in inappropriate behavior. Since a goal of the child-care worker is to build a strong relationship with the child, praise becomes an important component in accomplishing this task. Using praise also is important because many youth who are placed in residential treatment have very low self-esteem and do not see themselves doing many things right. Since praising the child is such an important aspect of the child's treatment, this model provides specific steps for the child-care worker to use so it is truly effective. Since the child-care workers can easily learn these five steps, they are more likely to feel comfortable praising the child. Using Effective Praise frequently can help the child realize that he or she does have many positive behaviors.

The eclectic-based University of Oklahoma program emphasizes the importance of a positive relationship between staff members and the children. This model does not focus specifically on praising the child as a way to enhance those relationships. Although the model cites the importance of developing relationships and improving the child's self-esteem, it does not provide clear, concrete, practical ways to accomplish this.

In a Positive Peer Culture, kids may receive spontaneous praise. But again, this would not occur because praise is a component of the program. Since this type of program is based on discussing thoughts and feelings, praise may occur as an emotional response but not as a result of a conscious effort to ensure that a child receives praise.

CHAPTER TEN

Corrective teaching/The teaching interaction

The youth who come to residential care facilities have had a difficult time living successfully in their families, their schools, and their communities. Many of them have been physically and psychologically abused. They have lived in dysfunctional and often chaotic environments. As a result, they have presented difficulties and exhibited problem behaviors that might have resulted in labels such as "conduct disordered," "emotionally disturbed," or "ungovernable."

Along with these problems, each youth also brings his or her special strengths and qualities. The goal of the Boys Town Family Home Program is to build on each youth's strengths and to remediate problems. Rather than viewing a youth as "conduct disordered" or "disturbed," we take the approach that youth need to learn a wide variety of

skills. Most youth learn societal norms and appropriate behaviors and skills by observing and emulating the many positive role models available to them. But many of the youth referred to residential care facilities have not had the benefit of positive, consistent role models, or when such modeling has occurred, it has not been effective in helping them learn. Often, their "reinforcement histories" have led them to develop behaviors that provide immediate gratification, but turn out to be very destructive in the long run.

Because the youth have so much to learn and "unlearn" in a relatively short time, frequent, direct, skillful teaching is the key to success. Teaching is the critical difference between real treatment and custodial care.

Through years of research, Boys Town has developed an effective way to teach children new skills. The Teaching Interaction is a nine-step process for dealing with youth problem behaviors and teaching more appropriate alternatives. By mastering and thoughtfully using the components of the Teaching Interaction, child-care workers can help each youth recover from the past and grow into the future.

This chapter reviews in detail each of the nine components of the Teaching Interaction. In addition, some special techniques and applications are reviewed to help you successfully apply your teaching skills as a child-care worker.

Before explaining and describing the Teaching Interaction components, however, it is important to touch on several issues related to effective teaching and how it can best be used to help children.

▶ Teaching versus control

Behavior management is not a cure-all. It is often used inappropriately, which tarnishes its reputation. Like any therapy, it can be misused.

There are three main areas of misuse. The first, which is most widespread, is the use of outdated versions of behavior management with very negative results. Control for the sake of control does not make anyone better, even if "Big Brother" thinks so. Jerome Beker (1992) noted that many formal behavior management approaches "focus more on control and attempt to impose external rather than internally derived standards."

Second, no matter how good the therapy is, it can fail when child-care staff members engage in power struggles rather than helping youth by empowering them to control their own behaviors. This is popularly known as "power tripping" a young person and is a process that is destructive to positive youth-adult relationship development. (Obviously, youth who try to hurt themselves or others initially need external controls as the first step in the development of self-control.)

Finally, in addition to the urge to control, staff members also may attempt to "get even" with their youth, rather than teach them, for offensive or unruly behaviors. Staff members may take credit for changes in their youth's behaviors or view their youth as less self-directed. In other words, staff members may begin to see their youth in a more negative light when harsh behavior-control strategies such as yelling or assigning unreasonable chores are employed, even when these strategies produce the changes desired by society. The remedy is effective training, consultation, and staff development.

The Boys Town treatment model has sought to provide youth with an enriching environment that facilitates change, yet encourages each youth to develop individually and with an increasing sense of responsibility and self-control.

Integrated throughout the programs at Father Flanagan's Boys' Home are staff development systems designed to teach techniques for interacting with difficult young people and their families. Boys Town developed its methods and philosophy of care and treatment by recognizing that problem behaviors involve antecedent and consequent reactions in the youth's environment (Coughlin & Shanahan, 1991).

Briefly stated, the objectives of the staff development systems within the Boys Town Family Home Program are to train staff members: 1) to consistently recognize and reward positive youth behavior when it occurs; 2) to correct negative behaviors, in a nonaversive way, when necessary; 3) to actively teach the youth prosocial skills for healthy family and community life; and 4) to intervene in crises in ways that are nonpunitive and mindful of the youth's legal rights. In other words, the skills necessary for successfully living with and teaching antisocial youth can be viewed as opposite correlates of the adult behaviors that originally trained the youth's coercive style. The emphasis is on teaching staff members to interact with these youth on a day-to-day basis in a manner that is positive and empowering. That prevents overly controlling staff behaviors that can escalate negative interactions. To accomplish these objectives, Boys Town staff members are trained to use specific interactive skills that are critical to their success with the youth in their care.

▶ Quality components

In the Boys Town Family Home Program, years of study and research have been devoted to the question of what constitutes effective teaching. It is clear that each individual's style of interacting is the most powerful factor in determining the effectiveness of his or her teaching. People who are perceived as warm, energetic, considerate, positive, concerned, and genuine are usually highly effective in any interaction because they are enjoyable to be with. These traits are learned through life experiences and can be hard to describe in objective, teachable terms. There are, however, a few observable behaviors that are generally associated with certain positive personality styles. These behaviors are referred to as "quality components" and include pleasant facial expressions, gestures or statements of affection, humor, body positions, etc. The degree to which staff members incorporate these behaviors into their teaching determines to a large extent how well a youth will respond to the content of what is being taught.

Direct, frequent, concerned teaching also helps staff members. Such a teaching approach provides a specific, effective, positive way to deal with problem behaviors. Because teaching is a positive approach that works well and is liked by children, staff members can avoid punitive approaches that could damage relationships. For example, Bedlington, Solmick, Braukmann, Kirigin, and Wolf (1979) evaluated several group homes and found that the level of teaching in a home positively correlated with youth satisfaction and negatively correlated with self-reported delinquency. That is, the more teaching the staff did, the better the youth liked the program and the less delinquency they reported. As staff members see the progress each youth is making, their commitment and sense of accomplishment grows.

▶ Teaching Interaction components

The following nine components and the various subcomponents comprise the Teaching Interaction used in the Boys Town Family Home Program to deal with problem behaviors and to teach youth new alternative skills and behaviors.

1. **Initial Praise, Empathy, or Affection**

2. **Description/Demonstration of Inappropriate Behavior**

3. **Consequences**

    ◆ **Loss of a Privilege/Point Loss**

    ◆ **Positive Correction Statement**

4. **Description/Demonstration of Appropriate Behavior**

5. **Rationale**

6. **Requests for Acknowledgment**

7. **Practice**

8. **Feedback**

    ◆ **Praise**

    ◆ **Specific Description or Demonstration**

    ◆ **Positive Consequences**

9. **Praise Throughout the Interaction**

1. Initial praise, empathy, or affection — Each interaction begins on a positive note with specific, sincere praise that describes appropriate aspects of the youth's behavior. To make such praise most effective, it should be behav-iorally specific and descriptive (see Chapter 7, "Recognizing and Describing Behavior"), and should be related to the skill that will be taught or to an approximate behavior. The descriptive, specific nature of the praise further increases the probability that those appropriate behaviors will occur again in the future. Praising behavior related to the skill has two functions. First, it increases the sincerity and naturalness of the teaching. Second, it reinforces approximations to the desired behavior and helps the youth recognize progress.

If the youth is not engaging in behavior that warrants praise or appropriate behavior related to the skill to be taught, you still can begin the Teaching Interaction on a positive note by providing an empathy statement. An empathy statement lets the youth know that you understand how she or he may be feeling.

Example: "Mark, I know how much you were counting on going on a home visit this weekend, and I'm sure you're really disappointed that you can't go," or "Boy, it can be really irritating when somebody breaks one of your belongings and doesn't tell you about it."

Such empathy statements can help build relationships, calm an agitated youth, and help you approach the situation in a positive, calm manner.

Initial praise and empathy also can be accompanied by verbal and nonverbal expressions of affection. Affection is an important quality component that can be conveyed by a concerned, pleasant tone of voice, a comforting hand on the shoulder, a pat on the back, a smile, or a statement of care and concern (e.g. "Mary, I'm really concerned about you."). Such expressions of affection enhance the overall quality of praise or empathy, and let the youth know that only his or her behavior is at issue — not the youth's relationship with you. (See Chapter 3, "Relationship Development.")

Without the consistent use of this component, youth could come to view you as a punishing stimulus — someone who is quick to criticize and slow to recognize accomplishments.

With the consistent use of initial praise, empathy, and affection, you can strengthen and reinforce appropriate behavior. You can build relationships by recognizing accomplishments and acknowledging feelings, and can help the youth be more receptive and open to the entire teaching process.

2. Description/demonstration of inappropriate behavior — This component involves labeling the skill that will be taught and specifically describing the youth's inappropriate verbal and nonverbal behavior. Labeling the skill is often accomplished by describing the antecedent conditions.

Example: "When I asked you to help with dinner, you rolled your eyes, sighed, and said, 'Oh, can't it wait until later' in a whiny tone of voice."

When behaviors are difficult to describe, such as voice tone, gestures, or facial expressions, you can demonstrate the behavior.

You should use the skills learned in Chapter 7, "Recognizing and Describing Behavior," to provide clear skill labels and nonjudgmental, specific behavioral descriptions. Descriptions of inappropriate behaviors help the youth understand exactly what behaviors need to be changed; the youth is not left trying to interpret or guess the meaning of vague terms such as "bad attitude," "defiant," "moody," etc. Descriptions of inappropriate behavior also help the youth understand the tolerance levels and limits that have been set. Without clear, objective descriptions of inappropriate behavior, a youth may not be aware of what behaviors are inappropriate and might continue using them.

To be most effective, descriptions or demonstrations of behavior should be given in a matter-of-fact, calm manner. You should be especially careful not to use harsh or accusing voice tones, and not mock the youth or exaggerate his or her behaviors. A calm, matter-of-fact approach makes it more likely that the youth will listen and learn. A belittling, harsh, or mocking approach is likely to result in an emotional reaction, and potentially, a confrontation.

In summary, clear skill labels and specific behavioral descriptions of inappropriate behavior delivered in a calm, matter-of-fact manner can help the youth more quickly learn expectations and behaviors that need to be changed.

3. Consequences — This component involves delivering a negative consequence, such as a point fine or the loss of a privilege, for an inappropriate behavior. Immediately following the consequence, you should offer a positive correction statement. A positive correction statement lets the youth know that he

or she will have an opportunity to immediately earn back some of the consequence by practicing a new skill or behavior.

Example: "For not accepting criticism, you have earned 1,500 negative points. You'll have a chance to earn some of those points back by practicing."

Up to half of the consequence that is lost may be earned back during the practice session. When delivering the consequence, you should take the opportunity to relabel the skill. You also should use phrases such as "You've earned..." rather than "I'm giving you...." Using the former phrasing helps the youth understand that it is his or her behavior that resulted in a point fine, not your behavior.

The negative consequence and the positive correction statement also should prompt you to remember the "4:1 Rule." The "4:1 Rule" means that for any misbehavior for which a youth earns a negative consequence, the child-care worker should provide at least four opportunities during that day for the youth to engage in the alternative positive behavior and earn positive consequences.

Immediate, calm delivery of negative consequences along with a positive correction statement helps discourage the youth from engaging in the inappropriate behavior in the future, and helps motivate him or her to learn a new skill. Without the use of negative consequences, you can actually reinforce the inappropriate behavior with your attention, teaching, and concern. The negative consequence provides a response cost for engaging in the inappropriate behavior.

4. Description/demonstration of the appropriate behavior — Following the consequence, describe the appropriate behavior that should replace the inappropriate behavior. This provides the youth with an alternative behavior. The effective use of this component is similar to that of an earlier step — Description/Demonstration of Inappro-priate Behavior. That is, it involves labeling the new skill and specifically describing the desired verbal and nonverbal behavior. Like the description of the inappropriate behavior, you may choose to model the behaviors that make up the skill. You also help the youth generalize the skill to other situations by explaining relevant antecedent conditions.

Example: "Whenever someone has to tell you 'No,' whether it's your parents, a teacher, a coach, here's what you should do," or "Whenever you answer the telephone...."

Such statements help the youth better understand that the teaching will benefit him or her in many situations and is not an arbitrary process. Descriptions of appropriate behavior also can be supportive and nonjudgmental if you avoid "I" statements such as "I want you to...." Phrases such as "What you should do..." or "Next time you can try to...," sound less judgmental, yet clearly communicate what behaviors need to occur in the future.

Clear skill labels along with specific, step-by-step behavioral descriptions increase the likelihood that a youth will successfully learn new ways of behaving, and help you teach effectively and pleasantly.

5. Rationale — A rationale is a statement that explains the natural consequences of one's behavior. (See Chapter 8, "Rationales.") Youth view child-care workers as more concerned and fair when they point out the benefits of learning a new skill or the benefits of continuing to behave appropriately. Short-term, individualized rationales help youth internalize what they are learning and help motivate them to change. Rationales also teach morals and values, and should be extended to include sensitivity to others.

Example: "Stealing not only causes more problems but also hurts others."

6. Requests for acknowledgment —
Requests for acknowledgment occur frequently throughout the teaching process. You should frequently ask the youth if he or she understands what is being said. These requests for acknowledgment take the form of questions.

Example: "Do you understand?" or "Do you have any questions?" or "Can you repeat that back to me?"

Requesting acknowledgment encourages the youth to participate in the process and helps you avoid lecturing. It also lets you know how well you are teaching and how much the youth is understanding.

To effectively use this component, you not only need to request acknowledgment, but also to be sure the youth verbally responds to the request, preferably in brief but complete sentences. In addition, you should continually monitor your own behavior to make sure you are giving the youth enough time to respond. You also need to make it clear that you are not asking the youth whether he or she agrees with what is being said, but

rather whether the youth understands what is being said. Avoiding requests for acknowledgment that could promote disagreement or arguing will facilitate the teaching process. For example, you should avoid requests for acknowledgment such as, "Don't you agree?" or "How do you feel about that?" Such requests for input are more appropriate for counseling sessions.

Frequent requests for acknowledgment help you avoid lecturing and provide the youth with an opportunity to productively participate in the learning process.

7. Practice — During this step of the Teaching Interaction, the youth is given the opportunity to actually demonstrate the skill being taught. This component is one of the most powerful and important aspects of teaching. The practice session provides the youth with the opportunity to develop new habits, and to become comfortable with new ways of behaving before he or she needs to use the new skill in a real setting. It also provides you with important information; it is the primary way you can assess the effectiveness of your teaching. Over time, you can become a better teacher by closely observing the success of youth during practice sessions and then making the necessary adjustments in your teaching skills to be more effective.

Practice sessions can be most effective and most successful for the youth when you clearly set them up and give specific instructions. For instance, you should clearly "set the stage" by describing the setting and antecedent conditions, and by reviewing the behaviors you expect from the youth during the practice.

Example: "Okay, Mark, we are going to practice how to accept 'No.' I'll walk into the room and you'll ask me if you can watch TV. I'll say 'No,' and then you'll look at me, and say 'Okay.'"

Sometimes practice sessions can be more successful if you use a hypothetical situation that is similar to the situation that led to the Teaching Interaction. This can be particularly helpful if the original inappropriate behavior involved an emotional or intense response by the youth. In such situations, you can set up a realistic practice that involves using the new skill, but that does not involve the original situation. For example, you've told a youth that he will not be able to go on a home visit and he has responded by swearing and arguing. While teaching the youth how to accept "No" for an answer, you would probably have the youth first practice the skill of accepting "No" by using a pretend issue (e.g. "Joe, let's say you're going to ask me to go to the gym after supper. When I say 'No,' you...."). While the issue is a hypothetical one, it is nevertheless realistic, involving asking permission to attend an activity outside the home or facility. After the youth successfully demonstrates the skill in the pretend situation, you would return to the original issue for a final practice and a successful resolution.

8. Feedback — Following the practice, provide enthusiastic praise, specific descriptions of appropriate behavior, and award positive consequences based on the skills demonstrated during practice.

Example: "Very good! You looked at me and said 'Okay.' That is the way to accept 'No.'

You've earned 750 positive points for practicing accepting 'No.'"

If further corrective feedback is needed, you should again describe the inappropriate behavior and the necessary appropriate behaviors. The youth then can repractice the entire skill or the parts that need improvement. The total positive consequences awarded for the immediate practice session or sessions should not exceed one-half of the original negative consequence. If more than one practice session is used during the teaching, you will need to adjust the positive consequences for practice accordingly so that the amount earned for practice doesn't exceed one-half of the original negative consequence.

Keeping the "4:1 Rule" (positive to negative ratio) in mind, use praise, descriptive feedback, and positive consequences to reinforce the appropriate behavior and improve the likelihood that the youth will engage in the behavior in the future. This type of feedback also demonstrates concern and support for the progress the youth is making. As a supportive mechanism, it contributes to the positive relationships that are developing between you and the youth.

9. General praise — You should remain supportive and positive throughout the interaction by praising the youth for a wide variety of appropriate behaviors. In particular, brief descriptive praise is provided for behaviors that indicate that the youth is paying attention and cooperating (e.g. looking at you, answering questions, listening, etc.). You should pay particular attention to those positive behaviors that have been difficult for that youth in the past (e.g. listening without interrupting, accepting criticism). If a youth has had difficulty accepting consequences in the past, you should reinforce the acceptance of a consequence whenever the youth is able to do so appropriately. Provide a praise statement or words of encouragement at the conclusion of a Teaching Interaction to express support and to end teaching on a positive note.

Example: "You're doing a super job of accepting this consequence," or "Remember in the future to follow instructions just like we practiced. Good job!"

General praise throughout the interaction reinforces appropriate ongoing behavior and increases the probability that such behaviors will occur in the future. Such praise also strengthens positive relationships between you and the youth, and keeps teaching on a positive, success-oriented track.

The following is an example of a complete Teaching Interaction for the skill of "Accepting 'No' Answers."

Initial praise, empathy, or affection

"Thanks for looking at me while we're talking, Bill. (pause) I know how much you were looking forward to the concert."

Description/demonstration of the inappropriate behavior

"When I said 'No,' you looked away and began to mumble."

Consequences

"For not accepting 'No,' you've lost your rec room privileges for the next hour."

Positive correction statement

"You'll have the opportunity to earn back some of that consequence by practicing how to accept 'No.'"

Description/demonstration of the appro-priate behavior

"Whenever someone has to tell you 'No,' whether it's a teacher or your parents, or me, here's what you should do...." (list skill steps)

Rationale

"If you can accept 'No,' appropriately, you'll probably be able to do more activities because people will see you as more mature and responsible."

Requests for acknowledgment

"Okay?", "Can you repeat that back to me?", or "Do you understand?"

Practice

"Okay, Bill, now we're going to practice how to accept 'No.' I'll walk into the room and you'll ask me if you can go to the gym. I'll say 'No,' and then you'll look at me, say 'Okay....'"

Feedback

"Great! You looked at me and said 'Okay.' That is the way to accept 'No.'" You've earned back 15 minutes of your rec room time."

General praise

"Nice job! Keep trying. I know you can do it."

▶ Special techniques and their use

An important part of being a good teacher involves selecting the appropriate teaching agenda for a youth's behavior. In order for a youth to learn from the teaching process, he or she must be attentive. Therefore, your first teaching priority is to be sure that the youth is displaying attentive behaviors and not engaging in behavior that would interfere with learning. This section reviews the importance of "attentive" behaviors and procedures for dealing with inattentive or disruptive ongoing behaviors.

Ongoing behavior

Ongoing behavior refers to any inattentive or disruptive behavior that occurs prior to or during teaching that interferes with the original teaching agenda. You need to help the youth replace these inattentive or disruptive behaviors with attentive behaviors that will allow the youth to benefit from the overall teaching process. Such attentive behaviors include looking at you, listening without interrupting, appropriately responding to requests for acknowledgment, and not displaying behaviors such as fidgeting, sighing, etc.

A wide variety of inattentive or problem behavior is ongoing. Such behaviors can be overt, or obvious, such as turning away, arguing or interrupting, or they can be more subtle, such as looking away, sighing, or mumbling. Such ongoing behavior might occur before you even begin to teach, and can occur or recur during the course of the Teaching Interaction, Effective Praise, or Preventive Teaching®.

Obviously, a youth will not learn very much if he or she is looking at the floor, mumbling, pouting, etc. Likewise, you cannot teach effectively under such circumstances. There are two basic sets of procedures you can use to help create a more favorable learning environment. These procedures involve giving brief, specific instructions and praise for compliance, or stopping the original teaching agenda to do a complete Teaching Interaction on the problem or inattentive ongoing behaviors. The latter procedure is referred to as using a Teaching Interaction within a Teaching Interaction. These two procedures are discussed in more detail on the following pages along with some guidelines to help you determine which procedure to use.

When a youth begins to engage in inattentive behaviors that interfere with the teaching process, one strategy is to pleasantly give a series of brief, specific instructions followed by praise for compliance (e.g. "Please stop sighing."). Such instructions also can be accompanied by empathy statements (e.g. "You seem a little tense. Why don't you sit down over here," or "I know it's hard to accept 'No,' but I'd like you to look at me."). Whether or not empathy is used, the youth should receive brief, sincere praise when he or she complies with the instructions (e.g. "Thanks" or "Great, that's better!").

Often, the youth will engage in several inappropriate behaviors at the same time or will engage in one inappropriate behavior after another. In either case, you should give instructions to help the youth gain control over the more overt behaviors first. For example, instructions to stop pacing or to sit down would precede instructions to eliminate more subtle behaviors such as sighing or looking away. Often, a series of four or five brief instructions followed by praise is needed before teaching can begin or resume.

The procedure of giving specific instructions and praise for compliance is particularly effective when you have used a lot of Preventive Teaching and Effective Praise to help youth with following instructions. It also tends to be more effective, like most procedures, when you intervene early and don't wait for or allow the inappropriate behavior to escalate. Pleasant, calm instructions, which are sometimes accompanied by empathy statements and always include praise for compliance, frequently help the youth refocus on the task at hand. This allows you to efficiently resume the original Teaching Interaction. However, a series of harsh, demanding, or vague instructions are likely to result in a confrontation (e.g. "Stop that! Get over here! Be quiet!").

Another approach to dealing with ongoing behavior is to clearly set aside the original teaching agenda and do a complete Teaching Interaction. After stopping the ongoing behavior, you can return to teaching the original skill. Take, for example, a situation where a youth has refused to take turns using the stereo. You begin a Teaching Interaction to teach the youth how to share. As you describe the youth's inappropriate behavior, the youth frowns, looks down, and begins to mumble. It's obvious that the youth is having a difficult time accepting criticism, and you may choose to set aside teaching the skill of how to share in order to teach the skill of accepting criticism. It is important to realize that this technique (a Teaching Interaction within a

Teaching Interaction) still must be preceded by prompts or brief instructions, and followed by praise for compliance, since the youth must be attentive if your teaching is to be effective.

Basically, when ongoing behaviors occur, you always should deal with the ongoing behavior first by giving brief instructions, followed by praise for compliance. Then decide whether to return to the original issue or take the time to do a second Teaching Interaction.

Providing brief instructions and doing another complete Teaching Interaction each has its own advantages and disadvantages. Giving brief instructions followed by praise might allow you to quickly gain control of the youth's behavior and efficiently continue the original teaching agenda. The disadvantage is that the youth has not been clearly taught alternative skills, been provided with rationales, etc. Because alternative skills have not been taught and because there was no response cost (in the form of a consequence), such behaviors might continue in the future.

Doing a second Teaching Interaction teaches the alternative behaviors or skill and might reduce the probability of such behaviors occurring in the future. This option also might increase the probability that prompts or brief instructions will be effective in the future. On the other hand, this process can be complex and is more time-consuming. Also, it can lead to a series of Teaching Interactions which can make it difficult to return to the original issue. However, no more than three skills should be "backed up," since such problems eventually end up as an issue related to following instructions. For example, in the earlier situation, you began by trying to teach a youth to share. Then the focus of teaching became how to accept criticism. If the youth then had difficulty complying with your requests while learning to accept criticism, you could change agendas again and work on following instructions.

Whether to use brief instructions or complete Teaching Interactions is a judgment call you must make. Your experience with each youth, along with the following factors, will help guide such decisions.

One general guideline is to use Teaching Interactions for ongoing behaviors that are more serious than the original teaching issue. For example, if you are teaching a youth how to answer the telephone and the youngster does not follow instructions appropriately, it becomes more critical to help the youth learn to follow instructions than to learn how to answer the phone. In general, the basic skills of following instructions, accepting criticism, appropriately disagreeing, accepting "No," and accepting a consequence should take precedence over independent-living skills and other social and academic skills. Without these basic skills, it will be persistently difficult for child-care workers to teach anything since most teaching involves following instructions, accepting criticism, and often, accepting a consequence. Therefore, Teaching Interactions within Teaching Interactions can become a priority when behaviors related to these skills occur as ongoing behavior.

Other factors that might indicate the need for full Teaching Interactions to deal with ongoing behavior are the intensity, frequency, and intent of the behavior. A youth who is displaying intense emotional reactions, frequent or persistent behaviors, or behaviors that are purposely disruptive to the teaching process, might respond best to complete Teaching Interactions. On the other hand, mild inattentive behaviors might be most effectively dealt with through brief instructions and praise for compliance.

One special case that always calls for a Teaching Interaction is ongoing behavior that involves the inability to accept a consequence. However, the procedure varies slightly from a typical Teaching Interaction. Since it would not make sense to give an additional consequence to a youth who has just demonstrated the inability to accept a consequence, the Teaching Interaction does not include giving an additional negative consequence for not accepting a consequence. Instead, the practice and feedback components of the Teaching Interaction focus on practicing accepting a "pretend" consequence.

After the youth demonstrates the ability to accept a pretend consequence, you can give an additional consequence for not accepting the original consequence. You also should provide a lot of praise and specific feedback, as well as rewarding the youth with up to one-half of the original consequence for accepting the second consequence. Finally, return to the original issue that generated the emotional reaction to the consequence and complete the Teaching Interaction.

The best strategies to remediate such problems involve the frequent use of Preventive Teaching and Effective Praise for appropriate behavior. (See Chapter 9, "Effective Praise," and Chapter 11, "Preventive Teaching.")

▶ Summary

In summary, the nine components of the Teaching Interaction can help youth make tremendous gains over time. While specific skills must be mastered to effectively use a Teaching Interaction, it is much more than a technical process. Effective teaching can only occur when there is a genuine concern for the youth and when there is a thoughtful, individualized approach to teaching. The Teaching Interaction is like any good tool. It is only useful when it is used by someone who cares about their "craft," who has taken the time and effort to become skillful, and who knows how, when, where, and why it should be used.

Another key to effective teaching is the ability to deal with ongoing behaviors that interfere with the teaching process. Your judgment and the severity of the behavior determine whether instructions and praise, or Teaching Interactions are best suited to help the youth.

▶ Model comparisons

Corrective teaching again focuses the treatment on the child's behavior. This typically means that the three models that focus on "thoughts and feelings" would not use this type of treatment strategy.

In both the Psychodynamic (Medical) Model and Cognitive Model, there is little or no emphasis on teaching the child appropriate alternative behaviors. The therapist would feel that the child's behavior would inevitably change once his or her thoughts and feelings changed. Because of this, the therapist would not consider it necessary or important to address these behaviors in treatment.

This also is the case with Positive Peer Culture. This type of program does not provide the child's peers with instructions for specific interactions. Instead, the peers expect a certain type of "thinking," and they challenge the child's thinking if it does not fall within these parameters. This ambiguous style of treatment makes it difficult to measure replication because each program probably would operate a little differently.

It seems doubtful that the Behavioral Model would use any form of corrective teaching, either. Since corrective teaching is an active form of treatment with the child, it probably would not fall within the structure of this program. The behaviorist focuses on teaching the child alternative behavior, but this probably would be done by changing events in the environment rather than directly interacting with the child.

Corrective Teaching is used frequently in the Boys Town program. As stated earlier, this program is very skill-based. The program has a very structured form of teaching, providing a step-by-step process the caregiver can follow when a child displays inappropriate behavior. This skill-based format makes it very easy to train people in the program and to provide consultation to caregivers. It also allows the program to be replicated easily since everyone should be dealing with a child's inappropriate behavior in the same manner. In addition, this specific form of teaching clearly states what is expected of the children, so they are more likely to succeed.

Although teaching is clearly emphasized in the eclectic-based University of Oklahoma program, the caregiver is not taught any specific teaching steps or teaching processes. This could make it very difficult to evaluate the program to determine whether the child-care worker is successfully disciplining behavior. Each worker would be teaching according to his or her own interpretation of the theories that are offered.

CHAPTER ELEVEN

Preventive teaching

To further enhance relationship development through teaching, child-care workers need to take a proactive approach to their role as treatment providers. Preventive Teaching — teaching that prepares youth to use skills in future situations — should occur frequently to promote the development of new skills, to prevent problems, and to increase each youth's opportunities for success. Preventive Teaching involves identifying skills a youth needs to learn, planning how to teach the skills, and conducting the teaching session.

The notion of "prevention," or Preventive Teaching, not only is a part of the Boys Town Family Home Program, but also of society in general. One example of prevention that occurs routinely is the fire drill. Fire drills involve having the occupants of a building practice locating alarms and extinguishers, and using exit routes. Such prevention reduces the chances of serious injury or death in a fire. Another example of prevention is taking a young child on a "safe walk" to school at the beginning of the school year. Before school begins, parents take their child on a walk to and from school. This way, they can teach the child the route and how to cross streets safely, and can point out "block homes" along the route where the youth can go for help. Such teaching improves the youth's safety and reduces anxiety for the youth and the parents. Taking the opportunity to review and teach about situations that will occur in the future can prevent problems.

▶ Benefits of Preventive Teaching

Preventive Teaching offers similar benefits for child-care workers and their youth. Many of the boys and girls who enter youth-care facilities have experienced a great deal of criticism and very little success. Preventive Teaching provides an excellent opportunity for the child-care staff to reverse that process. Not only does Preventive Teaching improve the youth's chances of succeeding, but it also provides the staff with more opportunities to teach. Those preventive opportunities are more likely to be successful and beneficial because they are occurring in the absence of problem behaviors. This means that anxiety and emotions are not at high levels, and the learning process is made easier by a comfortable, supportive, relaxed environment.

Preventive Teaching is a great relationship builder. Youth appreciate the inherent fairness, concern, and support involved in learning something new that will benefit them in the future. They also appreciate the opportunity to learn how to avoid inappropriate behaviors that will result in more difficulties for them. Their anxiety levels in actual situations will be reduced and they can approach new situations more confidentially and recognize and remit previous problems. In effect, they have the opportunity to experience success without having to experience failure!

Not only do the youth have the opportunity to comfortably succeed as a result of Preventive Teaching, but the success of the staff is enhanced as well. Indeed, the staff's job satisfaction and personal satisfaction are improved as a result of effective Preventive Teaching. Preventive Teaching helps avoid confrontations by positively and preventively establishing expectations and developing the youth's skills. Child-care workers can be more

relaxed and comfortable with youth in a wide variety of situations.

▶ Preventive Teaching: What, when, where, and how to teach

The practical application of Preventive Teaching techniques involves knowing what to teach, when to teach, where to teach, and how to teach. In terms of content, Preventive Teaching sessions can focus on basic curriculum skills, advanced curriculum skills, or preparation for a specific set of circumstances. Basic curriculum skills are the focus of teaching during the first few days and weeks that a youth is in a program. In Boys Towns programs, the Basic Skills are "Following Instructions," "Accepting 'No' Answers," "Engaging in a Conversation," "Greeting Others," "Accepting Criticism," "Disagreeing Appropriately," "Showing Respect," and "Showing Sensitivity to Others." By using Preventive Teaching techniques to focus on these skills, child-care workers help the youth become open to and comfortable with the process of learning new skills. The learning process is frequently reinforcing in and of itself and, thus, the teaching process becomes reinforcing. In effect, having the youth learn these basic skills makes the youth easier to teach. It also makes it easier to teach more advanced skills, such as being honest, helping others, finding a job, etc.

Basic and advanced skills help the youth develop a wide variety of family and community living skills. Most youth receive a gradual "education" in these skills from their parents and other adults through modeling, discussions, praise, and discipline. But the youth in many care facilities have not been a part of such a natural, prosocial education process. In fact, most of these youth have had an inconsistent and often dysfunctional education that has left them confused and socially inept. Frequent, specific Preventive Teaching is critical if these youth are to make up for lost time and lost opportunities.

In addition to focusing on basic and advanced curriculum skills that are used frequently, you also preventively teach to prepare youth for specific or special circumstances. Usually, such circumstances are identified because you know each youth's strengths and weaknesses, and can anticipate situations that call for Preventive Teaching. For example, if a youth is very withdrawn and shy and guests will be visiting, you would preventively teach that youth a number of social skills. These skills would include how to greet guests and how to engage in a conversation. Such teaching before visitors arrive improves the youth's opportunity to succeed.

Another example might involve a youth who has always had difficulty asking permission and accepting "No" for an answer from his or her parents. If the youth was going home for the weekend, you would use Preventive Teaching to focus on those two skills in order to prepare the youth for a more successful home visit.

Another particular set of circumstances that calls for Preventive Teaching involves avoiding confrontations or situations in which a youth loses self-control. For example, if a youth becomes verbally or physi-

cally aggressive or loses self-control when given criticism, you need to do a great deal of Preventive Teaching on the skill of accepting criticism. This type of Preventive Teaching occurs not only right before a youth encounters such antecedent conditions, but also in the absence of such conditions. In summary, any skill can be taught by using Preventive Teaching procedures and youth can be prepared for many potentially difficult situations.

Preventive Teaching occurs frequently for new youth in the program. One of the first Preventive Teaching sessions should include teaching a new youth about the program and its purpose. The primary teaching agenda should specify the basic curriculum skills needed to reside in the program, within a family, and in one's community. Secondary agendas include information about the educational community, daily living within the program, etc.

The use of Preventive Teaching continues as a youth grows and develops during placement. The focus of the teaching might shift from basic skills to more complex skills, and to preparing youth for specific events or circumstances.

Preventive Teaching can occur privately with individual youth or in small groups. Teaching an individual youth typically focuses on the specific treatment goals or special situations that confront that youth. Small group sessions, or teaching that occurs with the group as a whole, typically focuses on skill areas common to all youth. For example, if a group of youth is going to attend a social event, staff members might choose to review manners, conversation skills, and expectations with the group. Such group teaching allows the staff to more efficiently teach necessary skills.

There are three types of Preventive Teaching: Planned Teaching, Preteaching, and Preventive Prompts. These will be discussed in detail throughout the remainder of this chapter.

▶ Planned Teaching

Planned Teaching involves teaching a new skill at a predetermined neutral time, and uses a number of Teaching Interaction components. The eight steps of Planned Teaching are listed below.

1. Initial Praise

2. Explain the Skill and Give Examples

3. Description or Demonstration of Skill

4. Rationale

5. Request Acknowledgment

6. Practice

7. Feedback
- ◆ Praise
- ◆ Describe Behavior
- ◆ Positive Consequence

8. Future Practice/Praise

1. Initial praise — It is important to start the teaching on a positive note. Youth will want to participate in Planned Teaching more frequently and will be more motivated to learn when the opening statement is pleasant.

Example: "You really have done a fine job of accepting consequences lately, Sam. When you receive a consequence, you acknowledge the

person, you write the consequence down, and you ask to have your card signed. That's great!"

* Note: The previous example assumes that child-care workers sign or initial a document to indicate when they administer a consequence. In the Boys Town Family Home Program, the document, referred to as an empowerment card, becomes a permanent record of the teaching that occurs.

2. Explain the skill and give examples — Tell the youth what you are going to discuss and identify the specific skill area to be learned. The use of the skill in a variety of environments is described to help the youth generalize the skill to other antecedent conditions or settings.

Example: "I want to talk to you about another skill and that is asking permission. Asking permission is important anytime you want something. For instance, you should ask permission if you want to watch television, if you're at school and need to get something out of your locker, or if you're at work and need to make a change in your schedule."

3. Description or demonstration of the skill — Break the skill down into specific steps that the youth will be able to accomplish.

Example: "When you ask permission, you need to look at the person you're speaking to, get their attention by stating the person's name, and tell the person what you want permission for in the form of a question. Wait for an answer, and acknowledge the person's answer by saying 'Thanks' if you receive permission, or 'Okay' if you don't."

You may need to demonstrate the skill to make sure the youth understands. Demonstrations are especially helpful in communicating body posture, voice tone, facial expressions, and other behaviors that are difficult to describe.

Example: "Let me show you what I mean. Let's pretend you are a schoolteacher and I'm you. I'll ask you if I can go to my locker and get a notebook. You tell me, 'Okay, but be back in a couple of minutes.' Now watch for those steps we just talked about...."

You (playing youth): "Ms. Smith, would it be okay if I go to my locker to get a notebook I need?"

Youth (playing schoolteacher): "Yes, but be back in a couple of minutes."

You (looking at youth): "Thanks Ms. Smith. I'll be right back."

4. Rationale — Provide a rationale that describes how the new skill will benefit the youth.

Example: "If you ask permission to do something appropriately, you're more likely to get to do what you want, and you won't get in trouble for not asking."

5. Acknowledgment — Request acknowledgment from the youth throughout the interaction to ensure his or her understanding and participation.

Example: "Do you think you can remember those steps? Do you understand why asking permission is important?"

6. Practice — Have the youth practice the skill so he or she can become comfortable with it. Practice also helps you assess the effectiveness of your teaching.

Example: "Now I want you to try it. This time you ask me if you can listen to your stereo. After you request permission I'll give you an answer. Okay? Let's practice!"

Youth: "Would it be okay if I go to my room and listen to my stereo?"

You: "Yes, that would be fine."

Youth: "Great! I'll be back in 15 minutes."

7. Feedback

◆ **Praise**
◆ **Describe behavior** — When practicing a new skill, a youth will probably do some things well and some things incorrectly. After the practice, encourage the youth by descriptively praising things that were done well, and specifically describing incorrect behaviors. Reteach the portion of the skill that was practiced incorrectly and ask the youth to practice again. After each practice, feedback should begin with descriptive praise and should be given in a positive manner with a calm, encouraging voice and posture. Enthusiastically describe what the youth did correctly. If the youth is having consistent trouble practicing the skill, check to see that the steps are not too difficult, that they were described specifically, and that the skill is age-appropriate. After the practice, compliment the youth on his or her effort and arrange to practice more later. The practice should be brief so it doesn't it become punishing for the youth or you.

Example: "Nice job! You looked at me, made your request in the form of a question, waited for me to answer your question, and then said you would be back in 15 minutes. There's only one thing you left out: saying 'Thank you' to show that you appreciate getting to do what you want. Let's try it again and this time remember to say 'Thank you.' Do you understand?"

You can have the youth practice again and provide feedback.

♦ **Positive consequence** — Give the youth a positive consequence for practicing the skill. Positive consequences take the form of points or tokens, which can be used to purchase privileges like television time.

Example: "You really did a good job practicing and learning the new skill of asking permission. For practicing the skill of asking permission, you have earned 1,500 positive points."

8. Future practice/general praise — Let the youth know that you want him or her to practice the skill again. The second session should follow fairly soon — within five to fifteen minutes. Practices become less frequent as the youth begins to demonstrate the skill more consistently. After each practice, continue to provide descriptive praise, descriptions of appropriate behavior, and positive consequences. The interaction should end on a positive note with praise for the youth's participation and the positive behaviors that were evident throughout the interaction.

Example: "Thanks for taking time to practice with me. You looked at me during the entire session and you asked some good questions to help you understand what I meant. It's important that we practice the skill of asking permission again real soon. Let's practice again in about 15 minutes, okay?"

Here is an example of a Planned Teaching interaction using all eight steps.

Initial praise

"Mary, you've been doing an excellent job of accepting 'No' for an answer like we have practiced. You always say 'Okay.' That's fantastic. People are more likely to look for opportunities to say 'Yes' when they can."

Explain the skill and give examples

"There's another skill I want to talk with you about and that is how to disagree with someone in an appropriate way."

Description/demonstration of the skill

"If you disagree with someone, or want some time to discuss a matter, you need to remain calm and look at the person. Tell the person why you disagree in a brief, clear, objective manner, and use 'I' statements, like 'I don't agree because...' rather than 'You are wrong.' Then thank the person for listening to your point of view, regardless of the outcome."

Rationale

"If you can disagree and express your opinion in an appropriate way, other people will be more likely to listen to you, you will be able to get your point across easier, and you might get your way more often."

Request acknowledgment

"Do you think you can remember those steps?"

Practice

"Now, why don't you try it. This time I'll tell you that I think the couch would look better over by the window. You can practice disagreeing with me by telling me that you think the couch should stay where it is. Okay? Now what are those steps again? (youth repeats steps) Great! Let's practice."

Feedback

> Praise
> Describe behavior
> Positive consequence

"Great job, Mary! You looked at me the whole time and remained calm. You didn't raise your voice or make negative facial expressions. You stated your disagreement very clearly and you even used an 'I' statement. That was great. There's only one thing you left out, which is really important, and that's to say 'Thank you.' Let's try it again and this time don't forget to say 'Thank you.' Okay?" (repractice and feedback) Excellent this time. You've earned 1,500 points for practicing how to tell someone you disagree."

Praise/future practice

"Thanks again, Mary, for being so cooperative during this session. I'm really impressed with how quickly you learned this new skill. We'll practice again in about 15 minutes. Thanks."

▶ Preteaching

Preteaching involves reintroducing a skill that was taught in a Planned Teaching session just prior to an event in which the youth needs to use the skill. The components of Preteaching are presented here:

1. **Reintroduce Skill**

2. **Describe Appropriate Behavior**

3. **Give Rationale**

4. **Request Acknowledgment**

5. **Practice (Child-care worker's discretion)**

6. **Feedback**

   ◆ **Praise**
   ◆ **Describe Behavior**
   ◆ **Positive Consequence**

7. **Inform Youth of Upcoming Situation**

▶ Preventive Prompts

Preventive Prompts are brief reminders of a skill given prior to an event in which the youth needs to use the skill. The components of Preventive Prompts are presented here.

1. **Brief Reminder of a Skill**

2. **Request Acknowledgment**

3. **General Praise**

▶ Summary

In summary, Preventive Teaching builds relationships and fosters skill development. It can teach youth basic and advanced curriculum skills, as well as prepare them for specific situations or circumstances. By teaching youth the types of behaviors that are expected of them ahead of time, child-care workers can prevent problem situations and confrontations with youth.

Preventive Teaching can be done on an individual basis or with the entire group, depending upon the circumstances. There are three types of Preventive Teaching: Planned Teaching, Preteaching, and Preventive Prompts. Each is used at a different time to prepare youth for an upcoming situation. Preventive Teaching is a real key to youth success and to the staff's sense of accomplishment as treatment providers.

There are two important additional points to remember about Preventive Teaching. First, negative consequences are not given during a practice session. If a youth becomes noncompliant, end the Preventive Teaching session and start Corrective Teaching, showing the youth a clear separation between the two procedures. Second, it's very important to practice all Preventive Teaching sessions to perfection to provide youth with the best possible circumstances to learn and be successful, and to maintain consistent tolerance levels for the entire staff.

▶ Model comparisons

Preventive Teaching means setting expectations for the youth in advance. This way, a child knows exactly what is expected of him or her and has a much better chance of succeeding. It is important when working with children to make them aware of the parameters. Not only will they do better in social situations, but they also will view the adults as more fair.

A therapist using the Psychodynamic (Medical) Model probably would use this skill sparingly, if at all. He or she may occasionally explain to the child what to expect during therapy, but the expectations probably would not be very specific.

The therapist also may explain what might happen in certain situations the child could face, or what feelings the child might experience. It is unlikely, however, that the therapist would explain what behavior the child should engage in, or how the child is expected to act in different settings.

The Cognitive therapist probably wouldn't see any benefit in these explanations, either. He or she might do some preventive teaching about feelings and expectations during the treatment process, but it would not be skill-based or specific. This type of preventive teaching is important for the child, but it may not help him or her succeed outside therapy.

In Behavioral therapy, it also is unlikely that the therapist would do a great deal of preventive teaching. Since the therapist is focused on changing the antecedents to behavior or manipulating the consequences, he or she probably would not see the benefit of preteaching the child about what is going to happen and how the child should respond.

Again, the child is a passive participant in the treatment, not someone who has some control or participation in the treatment plan.

Setting up the child to succeed is an important factor in the Boys Town Model. Using this approach, the child-care worker takes advantage of opportunities to explain his or her expectations to the child ahead of time. This helps prevent problems that the child-care worker might have to deal with and sets the child up to succeed. By doing this, the child-care worker is increasing his or her opportunities to "catch the child being good." This helps to build strong relationships between the children and the child-care workers because the children see the workers as fair people who are trying to help them.

Boys Town's Preventive Teaching also helps the child-care workers set up opportunities for the children to use the skills they have been practicing. Then the child-care workers can spontaneously reinforce the behavior when it occurs. This helps the children to generalize their behavior to different settings.

The eclectic-based University of Oklahoma program states the importance of making children aware of what is expected of them. This is great for child-care workers who have the skills to do this. The model, however, does not provide specific training for child-care workers who do not possess these skills. For workers who have a difficult time identifying and relaying their expectations, just knowing that it is important to do these things probably will not enable them to accomplish these goals as well as they might like.

There probably would be little preventive teaching in a Positive Peer Culture program. Since the peers typically are reacting to the child's expressed thoughts and feelings, they probably would not see the importance of setting expectations or teaching the child skills ahead of time. They may use a minimal amount of preventive teaching, however, in setting some expectations for group behavior, such as rules for the group.

CHAPTER TWELVE

▌Intensive teaching

Youngsters in the Boys Town Family Home Program are remarkably responsive to the praise and teaching they receive, and to the relationships they develop with staff members. However, despite the staff members' best efforts, there will be times when a youth becomes unresponsive and unwilling to follow any instruction. In essence, he or she is "out of control" and the use of usual teaching procedures becomes ineffective.

When a youth is a danger to himself or others, is behaving in ways that can damage relationships, or has gone from anger to rage, your goal is to help the youth calm down so teaching can again occur. Intensive Teaching involves all of the teaching techniques learned up to this point. However, the procedures are used in different ways and at different times to achieve the desired outcome. And because of the nature of these situations,

staff members are required to notify their supervisor whenever Intensive Teaching procedures are used.

The most desirable goal is to avoid and prevent the occurrence of such behaviors and episodes. This chapter briefly reviews the general preventive procedures that can be used to minimize the occurrence of Intensive Teaching situations. Also reviewed in more detail are the four general phases of Intensive Teaching: the preventive phase, crisis intervention phase, teaching phase, and follow-up teaching phase.

▶ General preventive procedures

The key to dealing with out-of-control behavior is prevention! Prevention begins the first day you begin working with youth. By using the skills and procedures learned during training, you prevent out-of-control incidents from occurring. Effective Praise, Preventive Teaching, Teaching Interactions, dealing with ongoing behavior, using the Motivation Systems, and building relationships all contribute to youth success and a positive living environment.

Frequent Effective Praise can prevent the need for Intensive Teaching because appropriate behaviors are reinforced as relationships are strengthened. If youngsters are more frequently engaged in appropriate behaviors, they are less likely to be engaged in inappropriate behavior.

Preventive Teaching is one of the most important methods used to minimize problems. The only difficult thing is remembering to do it!

The benefits of frequent Preventive Teaching are tremendous for the youth and child-care workers. As a child-care worker, you can establish expectations and supportively teach and strengthen appropriate behaviors, all in the absence of inappropriate behavior. Youth are then more likely to successfully recall learned skills during more difficult or stressful times. Preventive Teaching that focuses on the curriculum skills of "Following Instructions," "Accepting a Point Fine," "Accepting Criticism," and "Accepting 'No' Answers" must be done regularly if youth are to learn how to control their behaviors.

You also should preventively teach the "five-second rule," which requires all youth to go to a designated area when another youth loses self-control. This rule removes youth from an area where they could get hurt, removes an audience that could reinforce the inappropriate behavior, and prevents copycat behavior from the other youth in the facility. Youth earn positive points for following the five-second rule during Intensive Teaching episodes.

Teaching Interactions and responding to ongoing behavior also prevent youth from losing self-control. Ongoing behavior refers to any inattentive or problem behavior that occurs before or during teaching that interferes with the original teaching issue. By setting clear limits, consistently teaching appropriate behavior, and intervening early to stop inappropriate behavior, child-care workers can increase the likelihood that youngsters will respond to these usual teaching procedures rather than escalate their inappropriate behavior.

Using the Motivation Systems effectively also helps youth maintain self-control and prevents Intensive Teaching situations. Consistently rewarding positive points for desirable behaviors and giving negative points for undesirable behaviors ensures that youth will understand the connection between consequences and their behaviors. The youth then know that if they start earning too many negative points, they need to start earning positive points by changing their behaviors.

Relationship-building is another key to preventing Intensive Teaching incidents. You and other child-care workers develop relationships as you praise and teach the youth, spend time with them, advocate for them, and demonstrate care and concern for them. In the process, each youth begins to form a special bond with the child-care workers. This means that your opinion of the youth becomes important to the youth. As the relationship grows, the youngster is less likely to engage in behavior that might disappoint you and is more likely to engage in behaviors that make you proud.

Finally, you can prevent Intensive Teaching episodes by remaining calm and keeping yourself under control during stressful times. Unfortunately, a large number of out-of-control situations are reinforced by the person dealing with the youth. If you become upset and begin to argue with or yell at the youth who is having a problem, the youth's inappropriate behavior may escalate even more. It is important to remain calm, speak slowly, and use a pleasant voice tone.

Effective Praise, Preventive Teaching, Teaching Interactions, dealing with ongoing behavior, using the Motivation Systems, and building strong relationships should be used together to create a positive living environment. By skillfully and conscientiously implementing these elements of the Boys Town Family Home Program each day, child-care workers can minimize and avoid situations where youth lose self-control.

▶ Child-care worker behavior

Before talking about Intensive Teaching procedures, it is important for you to realize that your behavior directly affects the way a youth behaves. You must remain as calm as possible, even though the youth may be highly upset. Depending upon the frequency and severity of the behavior, you may begin to feel upset or angry. These emotional responses can interfere with your ability to deal with the youth's inappropriate behavior. If you become upset, it reinforces a youth's inappropriate behavior and minimizes constructive teaching goals. Staying calm isn't easy. If a youth is yelling, making threats, or refusing to comply with instructions, you initially may respond emotionally rather than focusing on teaching in response to the youth's problem behaviors. If the goal of Intensive Teaching is for a youth to learn self-control, it is essential for child-care workers to model self-control. They should use a calm voice tone and empathy statements, respect a youth's personal space, and be patient. Patience includes giving the youth time to comply with instructions and not rushing from one step of the Intensive Teaching process to another. The goal should not be to control the youth, but to teach the youth to exercise self-control.

▶ Intensive Teaching procedures

Despite the child-care workers' efforts to build on each youth's strengths and prevent problems, there will be times when the youth will not respond to the usual teaching and treatment procedures. A youth's unresponsiveness may involve a wide range of behaviors, from being passive, withdrawn, or silent to showing noncompliance by arguing, complaining, or swearing. Problem behaviors may even include making threats or damaging property.

Despite the variety of problem behaviors, there is a common element that indicates the need to use Intensive Teaching — the youth is no longer following instructions. Regardless of the severity or intensity of the behavior, the same basic procedures can be applied to help the youth regain self-control.

To help conceptualize the process, Intensive Teaching procedures are grouped into four phases. The four phases are the preventive phase, the crisis intervention phase, the teaching phase, and the follow-up teaching phase. It is important to note that the transition between phases is not always clear-cut; rather, there is a general flow to the process.

The preventive phase involves a series of procedures that are designed to prevent the problem behaviors from escalating and to help the youth regain self-control by using usual teaching procedures. If the youth's behavior escalates to the point where he or she completely losses self-control, the child-care worker enters the crisis intervention phase. The goal of the crisis intervention phase is to calm the youth and get him or her to begin following instructions. When the youth is again responsive and attentive, the teaching phase begins. During the teaching phase, the child-care worker continues to strengthen the youth's instruction-following skills, then does Preventive Teaching and follow-up teaching on skills that can prevent future Intensive Teaching situations. The follow-up teaching phase occurs within 24 hours.

Preventive phase

The goal of the preventive phase is to give the youth a chance to stop the negative behaviors before they become so serious that the youth earns large point fines. The key to this phase is your ability as a child-care worker to get the youth to follow instructions and to prevent the youth from escalating the inappropriate behavior. In fact, many Intensive Teaching episodes are predictable and, therefore, preventable.

Keep in mind that all youth may have emotional outbursts at some point. When they do, you must determine whether this is an isolated event or a pattern of behavior, and decide how to respond.

Intensive Teaching situations are preventable in part because the antecedent conditions that often result in a loss of self-control are fairly predictable. Frequently, the antecedent conditions stem from a situation in which a child-care worker has corrected a youth. In these situations, the youth may have difficulty accepting criticism, accepting a point fine, or, ultimately, following instructions. Another common antecedent to Intensive Teaching situations is a youth receiving a "No" answer. (Antecedents may differ from youth to youth.)

Through experience, child-care workers learn to identify cues in youth behavior that may lead to Intensive Teaching situations. They also will learn what behaviors indicate a weakening of self-control (e.g. short, sharp answers; tight muscles; lack of acknowledgment).

Since Intensive Teaching situations are fairly predictable, behaviors that result from a loss of self-control usually can be prevented. Often, you will be able to resolve the situation without an escalation of the youth's behavior. Your behavior is crucial in helping the youth avoid a loss of self-control. If handled appropriately, your behavior can help to defuse the situation before it reaches the crisis stage. Frequently, the avoidance of a crisis depends on the skillful use of empathy and understanding, and giving the youth an opportunity to calm down rather than making the youth feel like he or she is being backed into a corner.

On occasion, a youth may have a series of difficult experiences that are not observed by the child-care workers (e.g. problems at school, difficulty with friends, problems on a home visit). If these problems have led to a high level of frustration or anger for the youth, a single interaction in the home or facility, or a few normally routine interactions with a child-care worker may result in a clear, immediate loss of self-control.

In these situations, several procedures could be used to help avoid a crisis. One general key to successfully avoiding a crisis is recognizing early that a youth is having problems and taking a preventive approach to deal with a youth's behaviors. At the first sign that a youth's behaviors are becoming inappropriate, you must decide what method of intervention to use. Normally, you would begin by saying something like, "It appears that something is upsetting you. If you sit down and calmly talk about the problem, I'd be willing to discuss it with you." This provides the

youth an opportunity to calm down and explain the problem. Many of the youth with whom you will be working do not yet have the skills to deal with certain emotional situations. Therefore, you may opt to use problem-solving or counseling if it appears that a youth is displaying uncharacteristic behaviors. For example, if a youth who normally handles most situations calmly reacts to a routine instruction with an emotional response, then counseling may be necessary. In these cases, by choosing counseling instead of confrontation, you can avoid an interaction that could damage relationships or escalate the youth's negative behavior. Good judgment and discretion are key elements in knowing which approach to take. Under normal circumstances, however, it is necessary to use Intensive Teaching techniques to calm the youth and maintain an appropriate tolerance.

If Preventive Teaching or Preventive Prompts to discuss the situation appropriately are not effective, the youth earns a point fine for the inappropriate behavior. The seriousness of the behavior should determine the size of the point fine. If the youth engages in ongoing behavior, a simple, firm instruction can be given (e.g. "Please stop talking."). Empathy statements also can be used to calm the youth. In particular, empathy statements combined with specific instructions are effective in resolving these situations (e.g. "I know it's hard to listen to criticism. Please sit down and stop talking. I want to listen to you."). If the youth begins to display important attentive behaviors, you should generously praise the youth and decide whether it is necessary to continue with the Intensive Teaching procedures. If the youth is able to follow instructions and accept point fines at this time, you should complete a Teaching Interaction.

However, if the youth escalates his or her behavior, it is necessary to continue using Intensive Teaching methods. Remember, this is a very difficult time for the youth. You should be patient and more empathic in these situations, and focus on helping the youth regain self-control. The amount of time spent providing empathy and instructions will vary from youth to youth depending on the frequency and severity of each youth's behavior.

If the youth's inappropriate behaviors continue, ask the youth again to calm down and discuss the problem. At this point, you may decide that giving instructions and empathy is not helping the youth calm down and regain self-control. Simply speaking, the youth's behavior is getting worse instead of better. At this point, the youth earns a second point fine (5,000 points) for not following instructions. If the youth calms down and regains self-control at this point, you can continue the Teaching Interaction for not following instructions and return to the original teaching issue. If the youth continues to engage in ongoing behavior, give the youth several empathy statements and simple, firm instructions. If the youth does not comply, the youth earns a 10,000-point fine for not following instructions. You should continue to empathize with the youth throughout the interaction. Every time you give an instruction, give the youth an opportunity to stop the inappropriate behavior and calm down.

At some point in this interaction, you must determine whether the youth's behavior is serious enough for you to invoke the five-second rule for the other youth. As previously mentioned, the five-second rule is a signal for them to go to a predetermined room or area.

If the youth still will not calm down, he or she would earn a final fine of 50,000 points for not following instructions and for losing self-control. Why give a 50,000-point fine if the loss of points has not been effective up to this point? Even though the youth may not write down the fine and is unlikely to change his or her behavior at this time, the point fine is important because it gives you a pool of points to use while working with the youth and is a response cost for engaging in some fairly serious misbehaviors. Because the youth has earned a large number of negative points, he or she probably will not have privileges for the rest of the day.

The 50,000-point fine covers the full range of the youth's inappropriate behaviors so no more negative points are given. After you tell the youth he or she has earned 50,000 negative points for not following instructions, the crisis intervention phase begins.

The steps for the preventive phase are listed in Figure 1. Figure 2 is an example of a preventive phase interaction.

The ability to recognize the onset of bodily tension, which often precedes emotional outbursts, and to teach the youth how to release the tension appropriately can sometimes prevent the youth from losing self-con-

Figure 1

Preventive phase

Staff behavior	Youth behavior
Preventive Teaching/Prompting	First Inappropriate Behavior
Consequence for Initial Behavior	Ongoing Behavior (e.g. 2,000 points)
Simple, Firm Instruction (pause)	Ongoing Behavior
Empathy	Ongoing Behavior
Simple, Firm Instruction (pause)	Ongoing Behavior
Small Consequence (5,000 points)	Ongoing Behavior
Empathy	Ongoing Behavior
Simple, Firm Instruction (pause)	Ongoing Behavior
Five-Second Rule (if necessary)	Ongoing Behavior
Medium Consequence (10,000 points)	Ongoing Behavior
Empathy	Ongoing Behavior
Large Consequence (50,000 points)	Ongoing Behavior (last consequence)

trol. Also, the severity and intensity of the youth's behavior will many times determine the length of the preventive phase. Child-care workers should remember to take their time and not hurry through the interaction. Quickly giving instructions and point fines may seem like badgering to the youth, and may intensify the youth's behavior.

Crisis intervention phase

During this phase, you work with the youth until he or she begins to gain self-control. No additional point fines are given.

It is important to stay calm, talk in a nonthreatening voice, and talk slowly.

Emotional control is the single most important factor at this time. Your behaviors during crisis intervention are very similar to those used during the preventive phase: Use a great deal of empathy and give specific instructions. During the crisis intervention process, you should continue to offer empathy, and praise the youth for approximations of following instructions and other behaviors as they de-escalate (e.g. "Good, you've stopped yelling. I know it's hard to stay calm when you're upset."). Positive correction statements also should be used to let the youth know that by calming down and following instructions, he or she will begin to earn back some of the points that were lost.

Figure 2

Preventive phase interaction

Preventive Teaching/prompting

Child-care worker: "Bill, I'd like to talk to you about something, but first I'd like to ask you if you remember how to accept 'No?'"

Bill: "Yes, you look at the person, say 'Okay,' and then if you don't understand why, you calmly ask for a reason."

Child-care worker: "Great. Now, what I have to talk to you about is going to be difficult for you to accept. But remember, if you accept 'No' appropriately, it will make it more likely that you will get a 'Yes' answer later. Does that make sense?"

Bill: "Yes it does."

Child-care worker: "Okay. What I'd like to talk to you about is your request for an advance on your allowance. It's not possible right now because you got an advance on your allowance two of the last three weeks. I appreciate the way you made the request and the reasons you gave, but this time I'll have to say 'No'."

Bill: "Aw, I really need that money. I was planning on buying a new CD."

Consequence for initial behavior

Child-care worker: "Bill, you did a good job of accepting 'No' by not swearing. However, right now you're whining. For whining when I gave you that 'No' answer, you have earned 1,000 negative points."

Bill: "You are so unfair I can't believe it." (Bill begins to walk around the room.)

Simple, firm instruction

Child-care worker: "Bill, please stop arguing so we can sit down and talk about your concerns." (pause)

Empathy

Child-care worker: "Bill, I know it is hard to get a 'No' answer when you really want something."

Bill: "You don't know anything about how I feel."

Figure 2 (Continued)

Simple, firm instruction

Child-care worker: "Bill, we are not getting anything accomplished this way. Please stop talking and come over here and sit down." (pause)

Bill: (in a louder voice) "No way I'm coming over there."

Small consequence

Child-care worker: "Bill, for not following instructions you have earned a negative 5,000 points."

Empathy

Child-care worker: "I know it's hard for you to follow instructions right now, but it's the only way we are going to get this problem solved."

Bill: "I am not going to follow instructions and you can't make me."

Simple, firm instruction

Child-care worker: "Bill, this is getting serious. Please stop talking and sit down." (pause)

Bill: "I'm not going to stop talking. I know my rights."

Five-second rule

Child-care worker (to other youth): "Guys, I'm calling the five-second rule so Bill and I can work this problem out."

Medium consequence

Child-care worker: "Bill, you have earned 10,000 negative points for not following instructions. If you stop arguing and come over and sit down, we can talk about the problem."

Empathy

Child-care worker: "I realize you're upset, but we can work this out."

Bill: "I can't believe how unfairly you treat me." (Bill is now yelling and is still walking around.)

Large consequence

Child-care worker: "For not following instructions, you have earned 50,000 negative points."

Descriptions of the youth's ongoing inappropriate behavior, along with descriptions of the desired appropriate behavior, are used to help guide the youth back to the point of following instructions (e.g. "You're walking around. Please sit down so we can talk."). As in dealing with any ongoing inappropriate behavior, instructions first should focus on the more overt behaviors such as walking around, yelling, etc.

As crisis intervention continues, the youth's behavior is likely to de-escalate and escalate several times. The goal is to have fewer intense periods and fewer periods when the behavior escalates. This results in more frequent periods of improved behavior and increased compliance.

In addition to offering empathy, giving instructions, describing behavior, and praising approximations of appropriate behavior, there are several other important factors to remember in order to resolve the situation. For example, during the crisis intervention phase, the youth may complain about how many points he or she has lost. Anytime the youth mentions points, you can respond with a form of a positive correction statement. In other words, offer empathy statements and indicate a willingness to help the youth earn back some of the lost points (e.g. "I know you've lost a lot of points and I'd like to help you earn some of them back.").

During this phase, it is not necessary to continually talk to the youth. If you respond to every comment the youth makes and try to fill in uncomfortable pauses or give too many instructions, the youth may view this as badgering. As previously mentioned,

this may serve to increase the youth's inappropriate behavior rather than decrease it. Also, any statement of praise or empathy must be sincere or it could further provoke the youth. Use brief, easily understood statements and appropriate pauses.

The youth may want to argue with you and set up a power struggle. The youth also may make demands (e.g. "I have the right to call my probation officer.") or accusations (e.g. "You're not fair to me!"). Don't be drawn into arguments or discussions of outside issues. The primary task is to help the youth regain self-control, and you must stay focused on that task. The best way to handle demands, accusations, arguing behavior, etc., is to offer some empathy, and indicate a willingness to discuss the issue, consider the request, etc., once the youth has calmed down. You then can redirect the youth back to trying to calm down (e.g. "You can make that phone call after you calm down," or "I know you're upset and I want to talk about fairness, but right now please...."). By staying on task, you can avoid side issues that will only prolong the youth's loss of self-control and disrupt the teaching process.

As you work through the crisis, maintain reasonable proximity to the youth. You should be close enough to talk to the youth, but not so close that you invade the youth's private space and possibly provoke a physically aggressive response. In general, stay at least an arm's length away from the youth. If the youth is walking around or leaves the room, you should stay nearby, but should not "stalk" the youth by following too closely. If the youth is pacing around a room, you don't have to track the youth; simply stand in a strategic location or move a few feet one way or the other to maintain reasonable proximity.

There may be times when a youth will escalate his or her behaviors to a point where you need to call a supervisor for advice and instructions. This might include a situation where a youth leaves the facility or is becoming a danger to himself or herself, or others.

If the behavior is serious, the supervisor should be notified at the first opportunity. Never make a judgment about the seriousness of a suicidal gesture or statement; personnel who are trained in dealing with such situations should immediately be notified. It is extremely important that you not leave a suicidal youth alone for any length of time. It is better to make a conservative judgment than endanger the life of the youth.

An Intensive Teaching episode is highly charged for the youth and the child-care worker. It is important that you control your emotions and behaviors during a youth's out-of-control episode. The youth may engage in many behaviors aimed at getting you involved in content, side issues, or discussions about whether you care about the youth. The youth may act aggressively defiant in an attempt to get you to stop teaching and leave. The youth also may act passively defiant in an attempt to get you to intensify your behaviors. In all of these situations, the youth is trying to control your behavior. The key to avoiding this is consistent use of the Intensive Teaching techniques, varying the procedures according to the youth's behavior.

Child-care workers should keep in mind:

1. They don't need to respond to the youth's allegations about fairness, etc. — the issue is the youth's behavior, not the child-care workers' actions.

2. They shouldn't try to "outtalk" or talk louder than the youth — wait for the youth to quiet down for a few seconds before speaking.

3. They should remain calm.

4. They shouldn't be afraid of short silences, but they shouldn't let the silences run too long.

The crisis intervention phase can last anywhere from several minutes to several hours or longer, especially when the youth is passively noncompliant. Eventually, the youth will calm down and begin to make some progress toward following instructions. You then can test the youth's instruction-following ability by giving simple instructions. (Be careful not to give too many instructions or give instructions that could provoke more negative behavior.) Before any teaching can be done, the youth must be able to display behaviors necessary for following instructions — i.e. looking at you, acknowledging what you are saying, doing the task, and checking back. You must remember that it may take some time before a youth has control of his or her emotions and behaviors. Once the youth is able to follow instructions appropriately, the teaching phase begins.

Figure 3 lists the steps for the crisis intervention phase. An example of a crisis intervention interaction is presented in Figure 4.

Figure 3

Crisis intervention phase

Staff behavior	Youth behavior
Positive Correction Statement (pause)	Ongoing Behavior
Describe Inappropriate Behavior	Ongoing Behavior
Describe Appropriate Behavior	Ongoing Behavior
Simple, Firm Instruction (pause)	Ongoing Behavior
Empathy	Ongoing Behavior
Repeat Instruction (pause)	Ongoing Behavior
Positive Correction Statement	Ongoing Behavior

* Keep repeating these steps until the youth regains self-control

Teaching phase

This phase begins when the youth calms down and begins to follow instructions. In the early stages of this phase, you should continue to deliver empathy and instructions, and praise and describe any appropriate behavior. During the process, tell the youth that he or she is beginning to earn back points for following instructions (e.g. "Great, you've really calmed down and you're doing a nice job of listening to me. You're already beginning to earn back some points."). However, positive point amounts are not specified or written on the empowerment card until after the youth is able to calmly and appropriately write the negative points on his or her card.

Once you are sure the youth is calm and can follow instructions, some important teaching occurs. Because the first task is to get the youth to accept and write down the negative points earned during the preventive phase, the first teaching agenda is to record the number of points lost. In some cases, you may want to do Preteaching, especially when a youth may react negatively to the point fines. Once you determine that the youth can record the fines appropriately, the fines would be:

1. Negative points for the original issue — the amount depends on the seriousness and severity of the behavior

2. 5,000 negative points for not following instructions

3. 10,000 negative points for not following instructions

4. 50,000 negative points for not following instructions

Praise for appropriate behavior is crucial, as is awarding positive points for accepting the point fines and following instructions. The first positive points the youth earns back can be fairly generous since the youth can earn back up to half of the points

Figure 4

Crisis intervention interaction

Positive correction statement

Child-care worker: Bill, if you calm down, you'll start earning back some points."

Bill: (stops walking around)

Description of appropriate behavior

Child-care worker: "Great Bill, you've stopped walking around."

Bill: (ongoing behavior)

Description of inappropriate behavior

Child-care worker: "You're still yelling Bill."

Bill: (ongoing behavior)

Simple, firm instruction

Child-care worker: "Please lower your voice." (pause)

Bill: (ongoing behavior)

Empathy

Child-care worker: "I know this is tough, Bill, and I know you're upset."

Bill: (stops yelling)

Repeat instruction

Child-care worker: "Please lower your voice some more." (pause)

Bill: (talks softer)

Positive correction statement

Child-care worker: "Good, you've stopped walking around and you've lowered your voice. You're beginning to earn back some points."

that were lost, depending on his or her behavior. The youth immediately may earn points for following instructions (actually calming down during crisis intervention), possibly for practicing accepting point fines and problem-solving, and for accepting the actual point fines. The points earned back during these first four interactions could total about 20,000 points. You then may choose to do more teaching and provide opportunities for the youth to practice following instructions, appropriately disagreeing, apologizing, and the original issue. Of course, what is taught depends on the youth's behavior at the time. The youth also could earn 10,000 to 12,000 positive points for practicing these four skills.

Finally, you should return to the original issue that led to the youth's loss of self-control and complete a Teaching Interaction. Figure 5 lists the teaching phase steps.

Follow-up teaching phase

Follow-up teaching occurs within 24 hours after the Intensive Teaching episode. The youth probably will not have his or her privileges during that period because of the large amount of negative points earned during the episode. Thus, you will have time to do some extra teaching that focuses on the youth's problem areas. You can have the youth practice the same skills that were taught during the teaching phase (following instructions, accepting point fines, appropriately disagreeing, apologizing, and the original issue).

You also should teach the youth relationship-building skills, such as volunteering, making positive statements, and giving compliments. It is important to reinforce any alternative appropriate behaviors the youth displays. You must remember that your teaching should be done positively and constructively, even though the Intensive Teaching episode may have been emotionally draining and uncomfortable, and you may feel like punishing the youth. The youth must be allowed to save face and continue his or her progress at the facility.

▶ General issues related to Intensive Teaching

The following issues and guidelines can help child-care workers prevent and manage Intensive Teaching episodes.

One aid to developing or adjusting Intensive Teaching strategies is charting the frequency, duration, and intensity of such episodes. This charting is particularly helpful for youth who are presenting persistent problems. Charting allows child-care workers and supervisors to detect slight improvements that indicate that strategies are effective. Often, these slight improvements would not be detected without charting and, therefore, child-care workers might discontinue or modify procedures that are actually working. Similarly, problems can be detected early on and informed decisions affecting treatment can be made. Another benefit of charting is that it helps child-care workers remain objective about the negative behaviors the youth is displaying; charting helps them remain focused on helping the youth overcome his or her problems. Charting frequency and duration is

Figure 5

Teaching Phase

Staff behavior	**Youth behavior**
Praise (pause)	Follows all instructions
Preteach accepting consequences (pause)	Follows all instructions
Write down negative point consequences	Follows all instructions
2,000 — Original issue	"
5,000 — Not following instructions	"
10,000 — Not following instructions	"
50,000 — Not following instructions	"
(Pause)	
	Follows all instructions (earns back points)
Discuss and record	
Positive consequences	"
Following instructions	"
Accepting consequence	"
(Small, medium, large, and role-play)	"
(Pause)	
	Follows all instructions (earns back points)
Role-play skills	
Following instructions	"
Appropriately disagreeing	"
Original issue (e.g. accepting "No")	"
Apologizing	"
Teaching Interaction on the original issue	"

fairly straightforward. The following scale of levels of out-of-control behavior is offered to help track intensity:

1. Noncompliance

2. Passive behavior

3. Verbally aggressive

4. Physically aggressive to property

5. Physically aggressive to people or animals

Such charts also can be shared with the youth so that progress can be reinforced and discussed. A positive change in frequency, duration, or intensity indicates improvement, which merits praise. Frequently, there will be improvements in more than one area.

Child-care workers also can keep track of the issues and antecedents that led to each Intensive Teaching situation. In this way, they can do appropriate Preventive Teaching and can intervene early in the chain of behaviors to help youth avoid losing self-control. Remember, the key to avoiding Intensive Teaching is Preventive Teaching.

When Intensive Teaching occurs, child-care workers should contact their supervisor as soon as possible, sometimes while the situation is beginning to escalate. It is a good idea for the person who starts the Intensive Teaching to stay with the youth while someone else notifies the supervisor. Supervisors may coach new child-care workers through the procedures the first few times they are involved in an Intensive Teaching situation.

In particularly difficult or lengthy Intensive Teaching episodes, child-care workers may spell each other in order to take short breaks. When this happens, it is very important that the episode is successfully concluded by the person who first began working with the youth.

Several other things to remember regarding Intensive Teaching are:

◆ Some youth have displayed out-of-control behaviors for years prior to coming to the your facility. This may be the first place where their negative behaviors are dealt with in a positive manner. Each youth comes from a different background, each with factors that have contributed to his or her emotional development. Even before the youth arrives, child-care workers will have done their "homework" by thoroughly reading a youth's file and talking with others who have worked with the youth. This gives them a thorough background of the youth's behavioral tendencies.

◆ The use of empathy statements has been proven effective in de-escalating emotional behavior. However, empathy statements should be used in many other situations so that they are effective in Intensive Teaching situations. Child-care workers who use empathy only during Intensive Teaching situations may not be viewed by their youths as sincere and may actually cause a youth to act inappropriately to get this type of attention.

◆ Child-care workers should not assume that a youth has learned self-control after an Intensive Teaching episode ends. Self-control is not a one-trial learning experience; it takes time to develop. During Intensive Teaching, the point fines do not act as a cure-all; they are simply token consequences used as a response cost for negative behavior. Skillful child-care workers are fully aware that with some youth, the occurrence of future Intensive Teaching episodes may be reduced in frequency or severity, but may never be eliminated totally.

◆ On a larger scale, the point fines act as indicators of society's response to a youth's inappropriate behavior. In society, such consequences may include suspension from school, incarceration, break up of family and personal relationships, or getting fired from a job. The goal of the child-care workers must be to teach this type of reality through the Motivation Systems developed at Boys Town.

◆ Child-care workers must be careful not to take a youth's behavior or actions personally if they are to help the youth overcome his or her problems. Although the youth may say some things that are offensive and hurtful, the goal must be to help the youth. Child-care workers, first and foremost, must teach the youth how to behave so he or she will be successful in life.

A number of unresponsive behaviors — from silence and withdrawal to arguing and swearing — can signal the need for Intensive Teaching. The common element of these behaviors is that the youth is no longer following instructions. By staying calm and following the necessary Intensive Teaching procedures, a child-care worker can help the youth regain self-control and learn to handle future situations without resorting to extreme inappropriate behaviors.

Intensive Teaching is only one component of the overall Boys Town Family Home Program. The success of these techniques has strong ties to the use of all other components. A facility that successfully uses these components is one in which the youth can see that staff members care for them and will be there to provide guidance during all situations, whether they are positive or negative. Effectively handling an emotional time like an Intensive Teaching situation can be a key to building strong, positive relationships. And, if the youth can learn self-control and proper expression of emotions, the chances for success after leaving the facility are increased dramatically.

▶ Summary

Prevention is the key to heading off situations where a youth loses self-control, requiring Intensive Teaching procedures. The use of Preventive Teaching and Effective Praise, and development of strong relationships with youth are just a few ways to accomplish this goal. Being able to recognize cues that signal that a youth is losing self-control also can help the child-care worker to respond before the situation gets out of hand.

▶ Model comparisons

At times during treatment, a youth can become upset, lose self-control, and, in some cases, display aggressive behavior. Each of the six models we have been comparing has a different way of addressing these situations.

A Psychodynamic (Medical) therapist's role usually does not include dealing with a youth who has lost self-control or is aggressive. Since this model is not skill-based, the therapist cannot do "therapy" with a child who is not totally cooperative. The therapist usually would not attempt to calm the child by using skills that help the child become aware of his or her behavior and alternative ways of behaving. Instead, the typical response in these situations is to either restrain or medicate the child.

In Cognitive therapy, the therapist typically responds to aggressive or out-of-control behavior in much the same way. Although the child is more active in this treatment process and does not need to be totally cooperative in the therapy session, the therapist typically responds to aggressive behavior with medication or restraint. Although medication can be very helpful in calming the child's behavior, it also can have side effects, including impairing the child's thinking process. Medication may be a necessary alternative for some children, but if behavior problems are the only symptoms, alternative behavioral techniques should be tried first.

In Behavioral therapy, the therapist would attempt to identify the antecedents that caused the child to lose self-control, and the consequences that are maintaining the behavior. The therapist then would try to set up situations to change these factors in order to determine what impact this would have on the child's behavior.

Boys Town programs employ a similar strategy. The Boys Town Model also trains child-care workers in specific skills they can use while the child is out of control. These techniques help the child to calm down and give the caregivers something to focus on,

which helps them to remain calm as well. This is extremely important during these crises because if the person who is working with the child also becomes upset, the child or adult could accidentally get hurt. Staying calm and working with the child to help him or her change the behavior is a positive alternative to medication or restraint.

Conflict resolution is clearly discussed in the eclectic-based University of Oklahoma program. It explains the theory behind anger and how the worker should deal with the child's anger. The program also provides specific strategies for dealing with conflict and resolving it. There is much discussion about the child-care workers' behaviors, and the verbal and nonverbal messages they send to the child. The program stresses the importance of appropriately resolving conflicts with children and provides specific strategies on how to do it.

In the past, Positive Peer Culture programs dealt with noncompliance and aggression by isolating or restraining the child. It was not unusual for children to be locked in at night, or "guarded" by their peers 24 hours a day. Public awareness has changed most of these programs. These programs, however, typically do not provide specific skill training for the youth who are "providing the treatment."

CHAPTER THIRTEEN

Youth rights

All child-care agencies assume considerable responsibility for youth in their care. These agencies become the parent, teacher, minister, and protector for each youth. In these roles, staff members have considerable authority as they regulate the movement, diet, acquaintances, experiences, etc., of the youth. They have considerable authority, but not unbounded authority. For example, the staff members take on the responsibilities of a parent and act in the place of the parent, but do not have all the rights and options of a parent. Parents can do many things for, with, and to their own children that legally, morally, or ethically are beyond the reach of any other person or agency. Yet, the facility staff still must successfully carry out the parental duties and responsibilities for youth in placement. Thus, in its role *in loco parentis* (in the place of parents), Boys Town and

other treatment facilities must serve the best interest of each youth in every way.

Organizations that care for youth have always had the responsibility of acting in the place of parents for the best interests of each youth. Sometimes, however, this has not been the case. Too often, abusive practices have been used to maintain order or to ease the burdens of operating a program. Too often, the individual youth was not served well. Because of public exposure of these abuses in the 1960s and 1970s, organizations were sued, state and federal regulations were issued, legislative bodies passed new laws, new licensing and regulatory requirements were adopted, and new professional standards were defined and implemented.

All of this activity was designed to ensure that each agency would indeed act in the best interest of each youth. Youth came to be seen as having rights. Given that the first court case involving youth rights did not occur until the 1960s, there still is considerable lack of clarity about the rights of youth in treatment. Some legal interpretations of these rights are very expansive, while some practices are very restrictive. Boys Town has examined and addressed these issues and developed a comprehensive system that aims to maximize the freedom of youth, prevent abuse, and foster humane, effective treatment. Our mandate is: "As much freedom as possible; as little restriction as necessary."

Boys Town has a commitment to provide a safe environment for each and every youth served. A safe environment not only is free of abuse, but is one in which a youth can grow spiritually, emotionally, intellectually, and physically. It is an environment that respects the rights of youth and employs the most positive, least restrictive practices in caring for youth.

The Boys Town approach to promoting safe environments has multiple components. These are:

Policies and procedures

Training in positive interaction styles

Ongoing program evaluation

Regular youth interviews

Feedback from outside consumers

Staff Practice Inquiries

Training in the rights of youth

All of these components are integrated into a system of youth care that has a major emphasis on the provision of safe, humane care. Information gathered through the use of these various components is constantly used to update and modify the program as it becomes necessary.

▶ Policies and procedures

A commitment to providing safe environments begins (but does not end) here. Each staff member should be aware of policies and procedures that relate to protecting the rights of youth. Policies and procedures emphasize the intent of the program and outline the procedures followed when potential policy violations occur. Policies and procedures set in motion other specific components.

▶ Training in positive interaction styles

All staff members are trained in positive teaching procedures to help youth change their behavior while respecting their basic dignity and freedom. (See Chapter 10, "Corrective Teaching/The Teaching Interaction.") They also learn how to promote positive relationships with each youth. (See Chapter 3, "Relationship Development" and Chapter 9, "Effective Praise.")

▶ Ongoing program evaluation

Administrators, supervisors, and direct-care staff members receive systematic feedback on program effectiveness through regular evaluation reports. These reports give all staff members insight into the quality of care provided for youth. Routine behavioral reviews on individual youth treatment programs, with a concentration on behaviors such as school attendance, school progress, referral behaviors, and treatment target areas, are a valuable method of monitoring overall program quality. One of the features of a humane program is the extent to which it succeeds in reaching its goals. Routinely reporting progress on important goals helps a program achieve its goals.

▶ Regular youth interviews

In addition to interviews conducted routinely during the supervision process, each youth is interviewed at least twice a year by persons who have no direct administrative links to the operation of the youth's facility. During these interviews, each youth is asked whether or not he or she has been mistreated by the child-care staff or others. Each youth also is asked to express his or her opinion about the pleasantness and supportiveness of the child-care staff and others. These questions provide important information regarding the atmosphere in the care facility. The emphasis should be on how treatment goals are reached and the methods used. Information derived from these questions can be used to improve staff members' interaction and communication skills if necessary.

▶ Feedback from outside consumers

Interested, involved persons from outside the facility — teachers, probation officers, caseworkers, foster parents, or family members — are another important source of information about the quality of care provided. Consumers are polled annually regarding their impressions of youth treatment.

▶ Staff Practice Inquiries

Any questionable staff behavior is followed up by a Staff Practice Inquiry. Staff Practice Inquiries are investigations into suspected inappropriate practices that are indicated in a youth report, a consumer report, or observation by other staff members.

All allegations from any source about less-than-optimal care are investigated thoroughly and promptly. The fact that an organization promptly initiates such an investigation makes it clear that it takes its protective role seriously. The procedure should investigate all claims regardless of their perceived validity or their perceived seriousness. Even relatively benign allegations are investigated to sensitize all staff members to the importance of maintaining high-quality standards.

It is the collective responsibility of all staff members to safeguard the rights of youth. Any suspected abuse observed by youth, staff members, or persons outside the program should be reported immediately to the appropriate supervisor or program director. When such a report is received, administrators should start a Staff Practice Inquiry. The youth and adult allegedly involved are interviewed along with others who might have relevant information. The facts are be established and conclusions reached as quickly as possible. Quick action is important so that any danger or discomfort experienced by a youth can be eliminated, and so that any unwarranted harm to a staff member's reputation can be minimized.

Efforts are made to maintain the highest degree of confidentiality possible in all Staff Practice Inquiries. Total anonymity often can be maintained. But sometimes anonymity cannot be guaranteed when a youth might be at risk. Relevant persons need some information during the course of the inquiry process. For instance, parents or legal guardians are immediately informed of any allegation. In cases where serious allegations are made, Child Protective Service agencies are notified so that they can decide whether to conduct their own investigation.

Another important phase of Staff Practice Inquiries is the debriefing phase. Verbal and/or written reports are given to persons who have the right to know about any outcomes. It is important that relevant persons are kept informed, not only to protect the interests of the youth, but also to protect the reputation of any staff members involved.

▶ Training in the rights of youth

All staff members who work with youth receive preservice training to increase their sensitivity to the rights of youth. Typically, this training occurs before staff members begin working with youth. Subsequent to the preservice training, staff members are updated through the supervision process and through materials and meetings provided by the administration. Staff members need to be provided with specific rules about what to do or not to do in youth-care situations, as well as with less-specific guidelines that augment the sound judgment required of any person involved in youth care.

▶ Rights: Rules and guidelines

Fourteen major areas regarding youth rights that are observed at Boys Town are outlined in this chapter. This list is not all-inclusive but provides an overview of the training content. For each of these 14 areas, there are both rules and guidelines. Rules are empirical generalizations, or "rules of thumb." Certain priorities are called rules because they usually are not to be modified. In the very rare circumstances when rules are modified, they are never amended without advance permission from a supervisor. Guidelines, on the other hand, are less explicit generalizations than rules. They serve as guiding principles around which staff members must exercise discretion and sound judgment, depending upon the individual youth's needs and the circumstances faced by staff members and youth. Guidelines are prudent practices under typical situations.

1. Right to nourishment

Staff must provide each youth with healthy food and proper nutrition. A major right of each youth is the right to healthy nourishment.

Rules:

1. Staff must provide three nutritionally adequate meals for each youth each and every day.

2. The three main meals (i.e. breakfast, lunch, and supper) should never be used as a consequence or sold as a privilege. A youth has a right to these because he or she is a person.

3. Meals should never be made intentionally less adequate, less tasty, or less nutritious for any reason.

4. Medical advice, written orders, and guardian consent should be obtained before initiating weight-loss programs.

Guidelines:

1. Staff should provide a wide variety of nutritious foods for youth, including ethnic preferences when possible.

2. Staff should avoid imposing personal food preferences (e.g. vegetarian or sugar-free diets) or fad diets (e.g. eggs and grapefruit for each meal) on youth.

3. Although snacks can be sold as a privilege under some state laws, nutritious snacks such as fruits or vegetables should be freely available (e.g. apples after school).

4. "Junk food" (e.g. chips, cookies, etc.) should be available only in moderation. Prohibiting "junk food" usually is unreasonable and unenforceable.

5. Staff should provide documentation of adequate nutrition (e.g. keep menus for six months).

2. Right to communicate with significant others

Staff should actively teach youth how to communicate with others. Healthy relationships with significant others are desirable for all youth.

Rules:

1. Youth have a right to seek advocacy or communicate with significant others like parents, guardians, probation officers, caseworkers, therapists, or clergy.

2. Communication with significant others should not be used as a consequence or sold as a privilege (e.g. because Johnny did not apologize to staff member, he cannot call his mother).

3. Staff should provide methods (i.e. mail or phone) for routine and emergency contact with significant others.

4. Staff should advocate for each youth's right to present his or her own case directly in any formal or informal proceedings.

Guidelines:

1. Staff can exercise reasonable control over the form (e.g. two long distance calls per month) or timing (e.g. call probation officer when youth is calm) of communication.

2. Control over the form, frequency, or timing of communication should not be unreasonable (e.g. even though a youth is not calm, he or she can call a guardian after reasonable attempts to calm a youth have been made. Thus, after three hours of discussion, it would seem prudent to let the youth call.).

3. Right to respect of body and person

Staff should use interaction styles that are pleasant and that demonstrate humane, professional, concerned care at all times. Physical intervention should be used only after attempts to verbally calm the youth have proven ineffective and the youth is endangering himself or herself, or others. Violence is always forbidden.

Rules:

1. Corporal punishment (e.g. spanking or physical exercise) should never be used to discipline youth.

2. Staff should use restraint as a last option and only when it is necessary to prevent a youth from harming himself or herself, or others.

3. Staff should avoid using sarcasm, labeling, or name-calling that would humiliate a youth (e.g. discussing John's bed-wetting at Family/Daily Meeting).

4. The use of curse words is never appropriate.

Guidelines:

1. The least possible force should be employed when restraint is required.

4. Right to have one's own possessions

Each youth has a right to possessions that fit his or her developmental level and living situation. Staff should respect a youth's right to possessions and create an atmosphere that supports the youth's ownership of personal possessions.

Rules:

1. Staff should ensure that youth do not possess dangerous items (e.g. drugs, guns, knives).

2. Staff should ensure that each youth has the necessary tools or equipment for school or work, and that he or she has materials that are similar to his or her peers (e.g. books, clothes, bedding, etc.).

3. Staff should never confiscate a youth's possessions (other than dangerous possessions) without having the youth waive his or her right to the possession or without intending to transfer physical custody of the possession to the youth's guardian.

Guidelines:

1. Staff can exercise reasonable control over the possessions a youth brings to the facility (e.g. no contraband should be brought).

2. Staff can limit the use of personal possessions to reasonable times or places (e.g. no radios played after lights out).

3. If a youth is restricted from appropriate use of his or her personal possessions, he or she should be told how to earn back the use of the possessions.

5. Right to privacy

Under the right to privacy, staff should ensure that each youth has the same rights that are typically afforded to people in society. Each youth should have personal living and storage areas. Each youth's right to physical privacy should be protected.

Rules:

1. Staff should not open a youth's mail or listen in on phone conversations without the youth's permission.

2. Staff should not conduct routine, secret searches of a youth's room or belongings.

3. Staff should not physically search a youth.

4. Staff can release program records only to a youth's legal guardian or persons who have written permission from a youth's legal guardian.

Guidelines:

1. Staff should ensure that privacy is available in each youth's living space and for his or her belongings (e.g. bed, dresser, clothes).

2. Public searches (i.e. announced and with the youth and one other adult present) for contraband may take place when there is probable cause to search.

3. Although mail should not be opened and read by staff, a youth can be asked to open mail in front of staff members when there is probable cause to believe it contains dangerous contents (e.g. a youth receiving drugs from a friend).

6. Right to freedom of movement

Each youth has a right to a wide range of experiences commensurate with his or her age and maturity level. Procedures that physically restrict movement, or consequences that prevent exposure to healthy activities for extended periods of time, are generally discouraged.

Rules:

1. Staff should not use seclusion or "time-out" procedures as a discipline practice (e.g. locked in a room or isolated from the group).

2. A youth should always be provided with options for earning privileges.

Guidelines:

1. Staff can limit a youth's movement to a given area and time (e.g. in school from 8 a.m. to 4:15 p.m., at home from 4:30 p.m. to 6 p.m.).

7. Right not to be given meaningless work

Staff should ensure that each youth lives in a learning environment where chores, tasks, goals, and privileges are meaningful experiences that enrich a youth's body and mind. Ideally, consequences for problem behaviors will have an immediate teaching benefit and should not be principally punishing in nature.

Rules:

1. Staff should never give "make work" tasks (e.g. cleaning a floor with a toothbrush, digging a hole and refilling it, writing sentences 500 times, etc.).

2. Procedures that are designed solely to punish should not be used (e.g. having a youth kneel and hold a broom above his or her head or forcing a youth to eat a ketchup sandwich for squirting ketchup on someone).

3. Staff members should pay youth according to the prevailing wage and hour laws for performing personal work for staff (e.g. washing a staff member's personal car) or for doing tasks that benefit the organization (e.g. working on the grounds).

Guidelines:

1. Staff can assign chores and tasks related to daily living that teach life skills or personal values (e.g. making one's bed or cleaning one's room).

2. Removal from typical adolescent responsibilities should not be a consequence for problem behaviors.

Note: Although a youth sometimes must be removed from activities, this should be done only when the behavior is so serious that it negates the benefit of continued participation.

8. Right to file material

Staff should make provisions for youth to know what is being communicated in Treatment Reports/Progress Letters. Written documentation should be consistent with daily treatment strategies and target areas. Good child care ensures that the youth is aware of his or her treatment goals and progress.

Rules:

1. Staff should not deny a youth the right to generally know what is being written in his or her Treatment Reports.

2. Staff should be present whenever a youth is reviewing file material.

3. Staff must ensure that all file material is secure and stored in a locked cabinet when they are not present to provide supervision.

Guidelines:

1. Staff may routinely have youth sign Treatment Reports or Progress Letters.

2. Sensitive file materials (e.g. psychological evaluations or social histories) should be stored in a centralized file. This makes it less likely that a youth will be exposed to confusing or emotionally laden material.

9. Right to interact with others

Youth should be taught skills that enhance their relationships with peers and adults. Youth also should be provided with ample opportunities to interact with peers of the same and opposite sex. Interacting with people is a basic right. Staff should monitor each youth's social contacts to assure that they are appropriate.

Rules:

1. Isolation should not be used as a consequence for problem behaviors (e.g. instructing other youth not to talk to a youth as a consequence for a problem behavior).

2. Staff must provide youth with appropriate opportunities to interact with the opposite sex.

Guidelines:

1. Staff may limit interactions between youth and some peers (e.g. youth with known substance abuse or sexual development problems may be limited in their interactions with peers with similar problems).

2. Staff may limit when and how youth interact with peers (e.g. no telephone contacts after 9:30 p.m. on school nights).

3. Staff may ask other youth to leave the area when they are working with a youth, such as in an Intensive Teaching situation.

10. Right to goals and privileges

Each youth should at all times have a Treatment Plan, commensurate with his or her age and development, that affords the opportunity to work toward desired goals or privileges. All Motivation Systems should afford the youth an opportunity to earn some privileges. Each youth should know the specific behaviors needed to fulfill his or her Treatment Plan.

Rules:

1. No youth should be given consequences that prohibit him or her from earning any privileges for unreasonably long periods of time (i.e. more than 24 hours).

2. Youth should have the opportunity to earn at least basics, snacks, TV, and one phone call every 24 hours.

3. Youth should not be given consequences without being told how they can remove the consequences and regain their privileges.

Guidelines:

1. Time-based consequences (e.g. consequences that last for a specified number of days) should be used only for very serious problem behaviors (e.g. car theft, shoplifting, etc.).

2. Staff should provide additional instruction and attention to youth who have not earned privileges for three days in succession (i.e. increased time encouraging and interacting with the youth).

11. Right to basic clothing necessities

Youth should be provided with appropriate dress and leisure clothing that fits their age and sex. Staff should ensure that each youth's basic clothing needs are met at all times.

Rules:

1. Basic clothing needs should never be limited as a consequence for a problem behavior (e.g. youth wears no coat as a consequence for losing it, or a youth is forced to wear inadequate or inappropriate clothing as a consequence).

2. Each youth has a right to the same style, type, and quantity of basic clothing that is provided for other youth.

Guidelines:

1. A youth's personal preference in clothing should be strongly considered by staff as long as the personal preference is not extreme in terms of style or price.

2. Staff can limit the style of clothing so that it is consistent with the treatment goals of an

individual youth (e.g. sexually provocative or gang-related clothing should not be worn by a youth).

12. Right to the natural elements

Each youth has a right to natural elements such as fresh air, light, sunshine, and outdoor exercise. Healthy outdoor activities should be a routine part of every youth's experience. Staff should ensure that each youth has the opportunity to experience the natural elements each day.

Rules:

1. Neither the natural elements nor indoor light should be used as a consequence (e.g. a youth should be able to get some outside exercise even when on a restricted Motivation System).

Guidelines:

1. Each youth should be provided with the opportunity for outside activities each day (e.g. walking on the grounds or playing in a prescribed area).

2. Staff can regulate the amount of time spent outside and the degree of supervision provided for each youth.

13. Right to one's own bed

Each youth has a right to a personal bed and a private sleeping area.

Rules:

1. A youth's access to a personal bed or bedding should never be restricted during normal sleeping hours.

Guidelines:

1. Staff may have youth share a bedroom provided that each youth has ample space and privacy. Each youth has his or her own bed area; there is no sharing of beds.

2. Staff may regulate a youth's access to his or her bedroom during nonsleeping hours or limit the privacy of sleeping arrangements when a youth is at risk (e.g. when a youth is suicidal).

14. Right to leave program

Staff must ensure that a youth is provided care in accordance with the reasonable wishes of the legal guardian.

Youth have the right to advocacy by their guardian, including the guardian's right to place or remove a youth from placement.

Rules:

1. Staff cannot prohibit a youth from returning home or going to another placement if such a move is requested by his or her legal guardian.

2. Staff cannot prohibit a youth from returning to a less-restrictive setting if it is determined to be appropriate.

Guidelines:

1. Staff may voice support for continuing a youth's placement by using rationales in a timely manner if a guardian wants to remove a youth.

2. Staff should not impede the orderly transition of a youth from his or her current placement to his or her next placement.

▶ Summary

Boys Town is very concerned about protecting and ensuring the free exercise of all rights and privileges of youth. The guidelines and processes described in this chapter provide evidence of this concern. However, success in ensuring youth's rights is not guaranteed by procedures alone. It also comes from the "sense of quality" that is imbued in each staff member. All staff members should understand that it is their competence in carrying out Treatment Plans and diligence in monitoring their own actions and the actions of others that makes the real difference. Rules, guidelines, and procedures are necessary, but it is the commitment to providing the highest quality care possible that affords each youth a safe environment.

▶ Model comparisons

Most therapists and child-care workers are concerned about protecting the rights of the children with whom they work. How much this concern is emphasized within each model seems to vary, however.

Psychologists and psychiatrists working within the Psychodynamic (Medical) Model must follow a very specific code of ethics. One of the purposes of this code is to ensure that the patient's rights are protected. Unfortunately, others who work within this model, such as the aides in a psychiatric hospital, are not bound by this same code.

It has historically been acceptable to use physical force to subdue patients in a psychiatric hospital setting. And in many cases, staff members receive little or no training. For this reason, these situations often become volatile and much more physical than necessary. Public awareness and pressure has supposedly eliminated the atrocities that occurred in the past. When visiting psychiatric facilities, however, one can see that many still rely heavily on physical force and restraint as their primary means of control.

This holds true for the Cognitive Model as well. Again, the majority of therapists working within this model must adhere to a certain code of ethics. You seldom hear of a therapist violating the rights of his or her patients.

As in the Psychodynamic Model, however, Cognitive therapists also use psychiatric facilities for their more seriously ill patients, and typically support the care and treatment a child receives at those facilities.

Behavioral therapists often have been questioned about the ethics of their treatment. There is concern that they tend to make their patients robotic, and that some of their treatment strategies are questionable. The most frequently questioned aspect of this model is the use of aversive stimuli. Its use often is debated, with the main concern being how far one can go "in the best interest" of the patient.

The Boys Town Model does not use aversive stimuli as a behavioral technique. Youth rights are of primary importance and are emphasized throughout the program. There is a strong belief that youth can receive more humane and ethical treatment from staff members using the skills described in this program. It has been determined that staff members who use these teaching techniques seldom have to use any type of physical force. In the Boys Town Model, a child's rights are always specifically described, and the staff is expected to respect and protect those rights.

Throughout the eclectic-based University of Oklahoma program, there is an emphasis on showing concern or respect for the child in care. The program implies that these children are to be seen as human beings and their rights are to be respected. The program, however, does not specifically describe what a child's rights are. Under these circumstances, staff members who mean well could violate a child's rights without even realizing it.

A youth's rights typically are not taught in a Positive Peer Culture environment, either. As stated earlier, isolation or restraint have been used in these programs, but these practices seem to have been reduced. Caregivers who use this program also need to monitor the youth to make sure they are not using tactics that could be seen as humiliating to the child receiving treatment.

CHAPTER FOURTEEN

Problem-solving

In addition to having major skill deficits, youth who come to a youth-care facility also bring with them a number of interpersonal, school, and family-related problems. And of course, as each youth experiences the normal processes of adolescent development, he or she will encounter personal problems that require solutions. To help youth resolve conflicts, plan for the future, and make decisions about how they will live their lives, Boys Town child-care workers teach problem-solving skills in one-to-one counseling sessions. This chapter reviews the goals of problem-solving counseling, child-care worker behaviors that can make such counseling work more effective, and the actual procedures to guide a youth through such a session.

▶ Problem-solving counseling

This type of counseling is like traditional, academic counseling with an emphasis on listening, empathy, and exploring feelings. You should not appear shocked by anything the youth say. It is very important to accept all kinds of feelings and let each youth know that it is okay to have a wide variety of thoughts and feelings. This helps the youth feel comfortable expressing his or her emotions, fears, and concerns about intimate or embarrassing events; this helps you to better understand the youth and put their current behavior in the context of those feelings.

In the Boys Town Family Home Program, counseling goes beyond the traditional exploration of feelings and seeks to work out new, more appropriate responses to feelings. This approach teaches that while it is okay to feel a certain way, it is not okay for a person to behave any way he or she wants because society holds people accountable for what they do.

Each part of the technique is important. You should not jump to the solutions stage before a youth's feelings have been fully explored. Problem-solving counseling involves actively teaching problem-solving skills while helping a youth arrive at a specific plan of action to solve a problem situation. Many youth problems develop as a result of poor decision-making. Problem-solving counseling can help youth learn to clearly think through an issue before making a decision and can provide you with the opportunity to guide the decision-making process. Also, such counseling is easy for youth to understand and more beneficial than more traditional approaches.

Your goals during problem-solving counseling sessions are to help the youth arrive at a viable solution to his or her problem, and to teach the youth problem-solving skills. Because such counseling sessions also promote and establish trust between you and the youth, another important goal is to build relationships through expressions of concern, affection, respect, and interest in the youth's problems. As a youth confides in you and sees that confidentiality is respected and met with concern and helpfulness, he or she will feel more and more comfortable problem-solving with you.

Problem-solving counseling is most appropriate when a youth needs to develop a plan to deal with a problem. The problem might be one that he or she is currently experiencing, or one that is anticipated. The problem might involve the youth's parents, siblings, teachers, friends, employer, girlfriend, or boyfriend. Problems can range from how to talk with a teacher who has unfairly dealt with the youth, to how to resist peer pressure, to deciding whether or not to participate in an activity. The problem-solving process also can be used to assess past problems so that a youth can make better decisions in the future.

There also are a number of situations when problem-solving counseling is not appropriate. These situations include times when child-care workers are trying to teach a youth a new skill. In these situations, Preventive Teaching, not counseling, is the appropriate procedure. (See Chapter 11, "Preventive Teaching.") You also should not problem-solve and counsel a youth when dealing with inappropriate behaviors such as skill deficiencies, rule violations, or inattentive ongoing behavior. Such youth behaviors require the consistent, concerned use of Teaching Interactions. (See Chapter 10, "Corrective Teaching/The Teaching Interaction.") At times, you might be tempted to counsel a youth who is engaging in behaviors that result from loss of self-control, especially when he or she is passive and withdrawn, or is complaining about unfairness. (See Chapter 12, "Intensive Teaching.") In such cases, it is important to stay on task, regain the youth's attention and cooperation, and complete the various teaching agendas. At a later point in time, when the youth is calm and his or her behavior is appropriate, you may choose to initiate a problem-solving counseling session.

There also are times when serious issues occur, and you might have to seek professional guidance in counseling. For example, you can help a youth work through a divorce or death in the family, but you must recognize that dealing with divorce and death is sometimes so traumatic that professional therapy is necessary.

A different kind of example is suicide ideation. This in itself is so serious that it requires immediate contact with the program manager.

In fact, anytime you feel uncomfortable with a situation, you should contact the unit supervisor, who will call on other qualified professionals to help meet the youth's needs.

In general, it is often beneficial for youth to go to someone outside the facility to discuss issues that are bothering them. It is only natural that a youth may feel more comfortable talking to someone other than you about some issues, even when those issues are not especially serious. This is because the child-care workers are in control of the Motivation Systems and, therefore, are in control of a youth's privileges. Sometimes, because youth are afraid of losing a privilege, they want to confide in another professional caregiver. You should feel comfortable having the youth rely on such outside resources.

▶ Counseling behaviors

There are a number of supportive counseling behaviors that you can use to successfully conduct problem-solving counseling.

These behaviors involve physical proximity, listening skills, and a variety of other verbal interactions. Each of these areas is discussed on the following pages.

Close physical proximity helps make the youth comfortable during the process. You should avoid sitting behind a desk or table, or having other physical barriers between you and the youth. Sitting next to a youth on a couch or in a chair directly across from a youth allows for physical proximity. Such proximity makes it easier for you to offer a pat on the back or a reassuring arm around the youth's shoulder.

You should avoid counseling sessions in the office area, which might be associated with consequences or negative events. If the office is used, sit on a chair next to the youth. If you counsel in a more public area such as the living room, you should do Preteaching with the other youth and ask them not to interrupt.

In addition to proximity, there are a number of listening skills that can encourage youth to discuss issues and express themselves. You can indicate that you care about what the youth is saying and respect the youth's input by looking at the youth, not interrupting, frequently nodding, and being attentive.

Your verbal behavior during problem-solving counseling sessions also can help the youth feel involved and comfortable. Offering verbal encouragement and praise (e.g. "It's really good that you're thinking this through.") can help keep the youth focused on the issue you're discussing. Asking clarifying questions and requesting more information reinforces youth involvement (e.g. "Tell me a little more about what happened after that," or "Can you explain that a little more?").

Providing empathy during the discussion lets the youth know that you are trying to understand his or her feelings and point of view (e.g. "That must be very upsetting to you," or "It looks like you're really angry about that."). Empathy is very important in establishing rapport with a youth and encouraging him or her to discuss issues.

While these qualities are important in problem-solving counseling, they also are important in day-to-day interactions with each youth. You should express care and concern, listen, offer empathy, etc., in everyday interactions as well as during counseling. There should not be a dramatic change in your behavior when you are problem-solving with the youth. Rather, nurturing, caring behaviors should occur on a daily basis. Because you consistently express your concern and act in ways that demonstrate your commitment, youth are more likely to come to you with problems.

▶ **Problem-solving counseling procedures**

The counseling and rational problem-solving process used at Boys Town follows the **SODAS-F** method, a revision of a counseling process developed by Jan Roosa (1973). **SODAS-F** is an acronym that stands for the following steps:

S Define the problem **situation**.

O Examine **options** available to deal with the problem.

D Determine the **disadvantages** of each option.

A Determine the **advantages** of each option.

S Summarize options, disadvantages, and advantages, and decide on the **solution/simulation**.

F **Follow-up** with youth.

This general framework for rational problem-solving has a great deal of utility and flexibility. The process can be used for group problem-solving or discussions such as those that occur during Family or Daily Meeting. (See Chapter 15, "Self-Government.") While using the **SODAS-F** method, you should use all the supportive nonverbal and verbal behaviors previously discussed. Each of the **SODAS-F** components is reviewed in more detail on the following pages.

Situation

The problem-solving process begins with you helping the youth clearly define the situation or problem. In some cases, the youth initially will present vague and emotional descriptions (e.g. "I'm sick of school," or "My folks don't care what happens to me."). You can use general clarifying questions or statements to help the youth more fully describe the issues (e.g. "Why don't you explain that some more."). However, it may be necessary for you to ask direct, specific questions (e.g. "Why are you sick of school?", or "Did something happen during your home visit?"). By calmly and skillfully asking specific questions, you can keep the youth involved and help him or her give a realistic description of the situation.

As you ask questions, you should provide statements of empathy, concern, and encouragement as the youth responds. Without these, the series of specific questions becomes more of an interrogation that can cause the youth to withdraw.

As the youth more clearly defines the situation, you need to summarize what he or she is saying. The summarization is particularly important before any options are discussed. The summarization helps ensure that all relevant information has been reviewed, and that you understand the youth's situation. If the summarization is inaccurate or incomplete, the youth can correct any misperceptions. This is especially important at this point since the remainder of the process is built around the defined situation. Without an accurate or clearly defined situation, it will be difficult to generate useful options and a viable solution.

Options

After the situation is clearly defined, you can help the youth generate options in the form of potential solutions to the problem. It is important to have the youth generate ideas that might solve the problem. You need to remember that the goal is to have the youth develop his or her ability to solve problems, as well as arrive at a solution.

To help the youth generate options, you can specifically ask how he or she might solve the problem or deal with the situation (e.g. "Can you think of a way to handle that?" or "What do you think you can do about this?"). After an option is suggested by the youth, solicit additional options (e.g. "Can you think of any other ideas?").

Initially, the youth might have difficulty generating options or generating more than one option. Also, the suggestions offered might not be very helpful or realistic. Whenever a youth gives an option, it is very important for you to remain nonjudgmental. You can do this by commenting positively about the youth's participation in the process (e.g. "Well good, you've come up with a second option. You're really trying to think this through."). You also can offer a neutral comment and a prompt for more options (e.g. "Okay, that's one option. Can you think of another one?").

Remaining nonjudgmental can be very difficult, especially when the youth suggests an option that would only result in greater difficulty (e.g. "I'll just have to punch him out."). You need to remember that your role at this point is just to get the youth to generate options. In that sense, this phase of the process is like "brainstorming." It is the next phase of examining the advantages and disadvantages that allows you to help the youth judge the "wisdom" of the suggested options.

During the option phase, you might give your suggestions, as well. However, this should be done only after the youth has given all of his or her ideas. You might want to phrase the option as a question (e.g. "How about talking to the teacher after class?") so that the youth still feels involved in the process. Over time, the youth will be better able to generate options and will be more comfortable doing so.

Disadvantages and advantages

After a number of options have been generated, you can help the youth think through the disadvantages and advantages. Each option is examined in turn and the advantages and disadvantages are discussed. In a sense, you are trying to teach that there is a cause-and-effect relationship between the youth's decisions and what happens to him or her.

As in generating options, it is important to have the youth think through the advantages and disadvantages. Again, your role is to skillfully guide the youth by asking general questions (e.g. "Can you think of any problems if you do that?" or "Are there any benefits for doing that?"). If the youth has difficulty thinking through the disadvantages and advantages, you can help by asking more specific questions (e.g. "Well, what do you think your teacher will do if you start a fight in his class?" or "Do you think she might be more willing to listen to you if you did that?").

There might be a number of advantages and disadvantages for any given option. Again, since a goal is to help the youth learn to think, it is important that you solicit additional advantages and disadvantages in this phase (e.g. "Can you think of any other advantages or any other problems?"). During the

process, you should remain nonjudgmental and not argue with youth about their perceptions of the advantages and disadvantages. This can be difficult when a youth seems enthusiastic about the advantages of an option that might not be realistic or could cause problems (e.g. "Yeah, it'd be great to fight it out because then he'd leave me alone and everybody would think I was bad."). Rather than argue about the advantage, you can simply acknowledge the youth's view (e.g. "Okay, so you think that an advantage would be...."). You can guide the youth's judgment later during the discussion of the disadvantages (e.g. "What happens if you don't win?" or "Could you get hurt?" or "What will your teacher do if he hears you've fought with another student?").

If the youth clearly does not see or cannot be directed to verbalize an important advantage or disadvantage, you should offer your viewpoint and allow the youth to react.

Summarize/solution/ simulation

After the disadvantages and advantages for the options have been discussed, you should summarize by reviewing each option and the associated advantages and disadvantages. This summary helps the youth see the cause-and-effect relationships.

You can then have the youth select a solution and prepare him or her to successfully implement it by doing "simulations" or role-play sessions. As a result of examining advantages and disadvantages, the youth typically selects a workable option. It might not always be the best option from your point of view, but it is more important that it is the youth's option. The youth is more likely to be committed to make an option work if he or she is truly comfortable with it and feels that the choice was his or hers.

After the youth has selected an option, encourage and reassure the youth that he or she can successfully implement the solution. To make the youth comfortable with his or her solution, you can answer any questions the youth has about how to successfully implement it. Another important way you can improve the youth's chance of success is to set up a role-play or practice session. These role-play sessions should be as realistic as possible. Often, you will know the people the youth will need to interact with as he or she implements the solution (e.g. parents, friends, employers, teacher). Because you know these individuals, you can simulate their behaviors. For example, if a parent is fairly abrupt and somewhat stern, you can best help the youth by portraying the parent in that manner. The role-play can be made more realistic by presenting the youth with several possible responses so that he or she will be more comfortable and more likely to succeed.

Follow-up

It is important that you express confidence in the youth's ability to implement the solution. However, you should not promise the youth that the solution will work. As the practice session ends, remind the youth to check back after he or she has tried to implement the solution. If the youth succeeds in solving the problem, you should praise him or her for doing so and for going through the problem-solving session. If the solution was not workable, you need to be supportive and

empathic. You and the youth can then return to the **SODAS-F** format, review why the other solution did not work, and find a more successful solution.

Learning to problem-solve is a complex task, but it is critical to a youth's eventual success. Because participating in the problem-solving process is so important, it would be reasonable to give the youth a large positive consequence or a special privilege. Also, because many youth have solved their problems in inappropriate ways in the past (e.g. running away, becoming aggressive), it is important to use positive consequences when a youth indicates he or she would like to talk about a problem (e.g. "I have a problem at school. Can you talk with me about it?").

The complete use of the **SODAS-F** format during a private counseling session is very important in teaching youth rational problem-solving skills. However, there are many other types of formal and informal activities that allow for the modeling and direct teaching of this problem-solving approach. For example, television shows and world events can prompt informal opportunities for discussions. As the youth express their opinions and points of view, it provides you and other child-care workers with some ideal opportunities to get them to think, to weigh options, and to discuss the possible ramifications of their views and values. Even everyday situations can create such opportunities. For example, a youth and a child-care worker might be riding in a vehicle and observe a young person driving a car as it speeds through an intersection, runs a red light, and squeals its tires. At this point, the youth might comment on how he can hardly wait until he can have a car so he can drive like that. The child-care worker can use this opportunity to ask if the youth sees any problems (i.e. disadvantages) with running red lights or speeding. He or she also could ask the youth for ideas (i.e. options) about how to impress people with a car without engaging in unsafe or illegal activities. Such informal discussions can help youth learn to think ahead, to get their needs met in appropriate ways, and to connect their actions with future possible consequences. All these behaviors are keys to thinking and problem-solving.

There will be more formal opportunities to use the **SODAS-F** method when a youth needs to develop a plan for the future. For instance, planning for his or her return home, a career, employment, college, or deciding how to develop an area of interest all lend themselves to the **SODAS-F** process.

There might be times when you will initiate a counseling session and use the **SODAS-F** process to help a youth develop a plan for more personal issues (i.e. making friends, personal hygiene, etc.). It is important for you to take a proactive approach to such sessions, as well as be receptive to sessions initiated by the youth.

▶ Summary

Problem-solving counseling has two important goals — to help youth arrive at sound solutions to their problems, and to teach them how to solve problems in a systematic, rational way. The **SODAS-F** process combined with important quality components

(i.e. empathy, listening skills, etc.) can help you accomplish both goals.

By successfully learning how to solve problems on their own, youth become more dependent and better able to assess and respond to different situations they will face. The **SODAS-F** method provides them with a framework for solving problems in a rationale, systematic manner.

▶ Model comparisons

Since children receiving treatment in the Psychodynamic (Medical) Model focus on remembering past events and discussing their feelings about them, they would have to do some problem-solving. This is crucial to helping them begin to understand why they have certain feelings or react certain ways. Typically, the therapist would model this behavior for the child, and encourage him or her to do so by asking the child certain questions.

The therapist typically does not teach the child a process for doing problem-solving on his or her own. The therapist also does not put much emphasis on using problem-solving for future events, since the whole focus of the therapy is on the past.

The same type of process is used in Cognitive therapy. Through modeling and questions, the therapist helps the child use objects to relive past situations and solve issues surrounding them. Once again, the child typically is not taught a process for doing this on his or her own.

Behavioral therapists, using a purely behavioral approach, would not see a need to teach problem-solving. Instead, they would manipulate the antecedents and consequents in a situation in order to teach the child to respond a certain way. They then can use repetition and reinforcement to get the child to respond consistently. They also attempt to provide settings in which the child could learn to generalize these responses in similar situations. The problem is that the child is not aware that these changes are taking place, and does not cognitively understand why he or she is making certain behavioral choices. This means that in settings where the behavior is not reinforced, or may even be punished, it is unlikely that the child will maintain the behavior.

The Boys Town Model combines behavioral techniques with teaching the child a process for solving problems on his or her own. This helps the child develop the skill of thinking through the pros and cons of a situation even if immediate reinforcement for the appropriate behavior is not available. It also helps the child to cognitively understand how this situation relates to other similar situations, and what consequences could result from certain behavior.

The eclectic-based University of Oklahoma program is somewhat similar to the Boys Town program. It also emphasizes relationship-building and a behavioral approach to discipline. It does not, however, teach the child an actual process for solving problems. Without a process, it could be very difficult for a child to think through all the advantages and disadvantages of a decision in different situations.

Problem-solving could very well be modeled in a Positive Peer Culture. This would seem to occur naturally, with the child's choices and decisions being challenged and questioned by peers. But the child is not taught to do this for himself or herself, so it is questionable whether the child could continue to use problem-solving when faced with situations outside the Positive Peer Culture environment.

CHAPTER FIFTEEN

Self-government

The Self-Government System of the Boys Town Family Home Program provides an opportunity for the youth to participate in decisions that affect their lives. There are three components to the Self-Government System: Family or Daily Meeting (Family Meeting in home settings, Daily Meeting in shelters), Reporting Problems, and the Manager System. Each of these components will be discussed in this chapter.

▶ Family or Daily Meeting

The Family or Daily Meeting is a meeting of all youth and child-care workers that is held each day, usually after the evening meal. A typical meeting lasts about 10 to 20 minutes, and its purpose is to involve the youth in decisions that affect the group or family. (To simplify reading, meetings will be referred to as Daily Meetings for the rest of the chapter.)

To accomplish this, child-care workers set general goals for Daily Meetings. The first goal is to teach the youth rational problem-solving skills. This involves teaching youth to define a problem situation, examine the options available to deal with the problem, determine the advantages and disadvantages of each option, and vote to decide on the option that appears to be the best solution. This problem-solving approach is called **SODAS-F**; it teaches youth to consider the pros and cons of a situation before arriving at a rational conclusion. (Chapter 14, "Problem-Solving" thoroughly reviews the **SODAS-F** process.) The second goal is to share positive events, problems, and solutions. Child-care workers should make the Daily Meeting as reinforcing as possible. They do this by scheduling the meeting so it does not interfere with privilege time, by giving the youth a chance to actually decide real issues regarding the home or facility, and by sharing positive information about the youth (e.g. school commendations, perfect school attendance).

Third, child-care workers use Daily Meetings to teach morality and values. When using the **SODAS-F** process, the discussion of disadvantages and advantages often involves morals and values, especially when discussing controversial topics (e.g. legalizing marijuana, movies with violent themes, etc.). These discussions present many opportunities for child-care workers to have the youth consider and discuss the moral issues and social values involved in making decisions. Finally, Daily Meetings help to teach self-government as a social ideal. These meetings provide youth with an opportunity to make decisions based on rational discussion and voting. They are a way for youth to appropriately disagree with home or facility rules or staff practices, or to discuss issues that interest or bother them. The youth learn firsthand what it is like to participate in a self-governing system.

Child-care workers also benefit from Daily Meetings. With an opportunity to contribute to the program, the youth are happier and more satisfied; this means fewer Intensive Teaching situations and less need for Teaching Interactions. Also, by using Motivation Systems during Daily Meetings, child-care workers can teach and reinforce the youth's rational problem-solving skills. This makes their jobs a lot easier because the youth learn to deal with their own problems with less direct staff intervention. The youth also appreciate the problem-solving skills they learn during Daily Meetings. Listening to other people's ideas and learning concepts like fairness, effectiveness, pleasantness, and concern during the discussions at Daily Meeting helps each youth come to understand rational methods of making decisions.

Functions of Daily Meeting

The functions of a Daily Meeting depend upon the skill level of the child-care worker who conducts the meeting. At Boys Town facilities, a child-care worker who has just joined the staff initially focuses on basic functions, and more complex functions are added after a few months. Basic functions include:

1. Teaching self-government skills — Most youth who have been in the program for awhile will have learned many of these skills. However, new youth need to be taught and the more experienced youth need to be reminded of the basic self-government skills such as decision-making, discussing rules, voting, etc.

2. Reviewing and praising progress — The staff should use Effective Praise to point out accomplishments, awards, and progress toward goals, as well as progress toward greater levels of self-government. This can help make the Daily Meeting very reinforcing for the youth.

3. Making announcements — The Daily Meeting is a convenient time to announce special events and discuss items that might affect the entire "group" (e.g. visitors to the program).

4. Planning group or facility activities — Staff members and youth should discuss options and make decisions about recreational activities.

5. Giving and accepting criticism (peers) — The Daily Meeting is a good setting for the youth to practice giving critical feedback to their peers and practice accepting feedback from them. This practice is important for developing the skills involved in such interactions, as well as developing and maintaining peer relationships within the program.

6. Establishing or changing rules — Reviewing current rules and modifying them as needed, establishing new rules to help solve current problems, discussing the rationales for rules to see if old rules need to be discarded, and so on all are good topics for Daily Meeting, and permit the youth to have an important voice in the operation of the program.

After child-care workers become skilled in these six areas of Daily Meeting, the next five functions are added with the help and advice of their consultant or supervisor:

7. Giving feedback to staff members — This is a very important function but it is often difficult to achieve. Staff members need to teach the youth how and when to give them feedback, and need to practice this skill with the youngsters thoroughly to make sure each youth is comfortable with it. Staff members also should ask for feedback often, reinforce constructive feedback when it is given, respond to the feedback appropriately, and when reasonable, change their own behaviors in response to the feedback. Over time, this will encourage the youth to provide constructive feedback.

8. Discussing and helping set consequences — This applies to situations where the youth could discuss and vote on the consequences that should be given for rule violations. Often, staff members tell the youth in advance what an acceptable range would be. The youth then vote to establish a consequence within that range. Rule violations that might jeopardize a youth's placement are not discussed. Consequences for those violations can be set only by the staff after discussions with the supervisor and program director.

9. Evaluating the manager — The manager is a youth in the program who is given certain limited supervisory responsibilities over the other youth. (The Manager System is described later in this chapter.) An important part of the Manager System is the review function that occurs at Daily Meeting. During the review, each youth has an opportunity to comment on the manager's performance that day. The manager then earns positive or negative consequences based upon this peer evaluation.

10. Evaluating consequences — This involves decisions on consequences for violations of new rules or other rules that may be discussed. Staff members should keep track of rule violations and negative consequences for a week or two and report that information at the Daily Meeting. If the rule violations still occur frequently, the staff and youth can discuss how to adjust the frequency of Teaching Interactions and the size of consequences to solve the problem. If rule violations are at an acceptably low level, staff members can use Effective Praise to reinforce such exemplary behavior.

11. Discussing grievances — Youth can bring up and discuss what they feel are unfair consequences or rules, and appeal to other youth and the staff for changes. This might include appealing consequences for violations of program rules, as well as individual consequences administered by the staff. By being allowed to question the consequences staff members give, the youth understand that the staff and the program are fair. Staff members should, however, approve whether or not a grievance is appropriate for Daily Meeting discussion. Some issues are private and should not become group issues.

Skills to teach for Daily Meeting

Child-care workers must teach the youth a variety of skills in order to have productive Daily Meetings. These skills usually can be taught individually using Planned Teaching. However, if enough youth need to learn or review the same skill, group teaching can be done. This might involve having a Daily Meeting specifically to teach the youth as a group, and having each youth practice some of the skills being taught. Whether they are taught individually or as a group, each youth needs to learn the following Daily Meeting skills:

1. Discussion skills — Eye contact with the speaker, acknowledgment (physical and verbal), not interrupting, asking questions, taking turns speaking, attending to prompts and cues, sitting up straight, and speaking calmly all are helpful behaviors to teach as part of this skill.

2. Criticism skills — Giving feedback, accepting feedback, eye contact, acknowledgment, not arguing, pleasant voice tone, appropriate disagreement, and offering solutions are components of this skill.

3. Giving rationales for rules and consequences — Rationales provided by the youth and staff are very important in helping the youth learn why rules are necessary and why consequences are used to correct or reinforce behavior.

4. Recognizing positive and problem behaviors — The youth need to learn which behaviors are important, to recognize those behaviors when they occur, and how to comment on those behaviors at Daily Meeting. This helps each youth know what is right and wrong, and helps to increase the value of Effective Praise or criticism that is offered by one youth to another.

5. Making rational suggestions — Initially, staff members might want to reinforce a youth for making any suggestions at all. Over time, they should teach the youth to make rational and reasonable suggestions. If a suggestion does not make sense or is not very rational, the staff can ask the youth to research the topic for possible advantages and disadvantages of the option suggested. This can be an educational experience for the youth as he or she discovers the reasons why the original suggestion did not make a lot of sense. Alternatively, the staff could choose to directly teach the youth how to make more rational and reasonable suggestions.

6. Learning concepts — During each discussion at a Family Meeting, staff members need to talk about the concepts of fairness, pleasantness, effectiveness, and concern so the youth will learn what these concepts mean. Staff members also can ask the youth how they thought the discussions were fair, pleasant, etc., to make sure they understand these concepts thoroughly.

7. Reporting problems — The youth not only need to learn to recognize appropriate and inappropriate behavior, but also need to learn to report it to the staff. When a youth sees something that needs to be changed, he or she should fill out a Daily Meeting card (explained on pages 165-166) and discuss the topic at Daily Meeting. They should understand that everyone in the program shares a reputation that can be affected by any one person's appropriate or inappropriate behavior. Thus, it is important to report problems and deal with such issues at Daily Meeting.

How to teach Daily Meeting behavior

With Daily Meeting behaviors, as with other important skills, Preteaching is very important. Staff members should use the first few meetings that include new youth to talk about these expectations for Daily Meeting behavior: how to get a staff member's attention (e.g. hold up a hand), how to bring up issues (e.g. fill out a card, then see a staff member), etc. After teaching these skills, a staff member can start the next Daily Meeting by going around the table and asking each youth to state one or two of these expectations. This serves as a nice reminder for everyone and helps reinforce those expectations.

Similarly, the reasons why Daily Meetings are important and why there are limits on the discussion topics can be reinforced by asking the youth to state those reasons at the beginning of each meeting. Limits on topics for discussion generally involve being sensitive to a youth who has serious problems. Drugs, sex, bed-wetting, or similar issues of a highly sensitive and personal nature may be discussed in general at a Daily Meeting, but the names of any youth who have, or have had, that problem should never be included. The staff should always handle such problems privately to avoid exposure or embarrassment that might upset a youth. Also, topics that involve laws (e.g. no alcohol for minors), program rules (e.g. no smoking outside or in any public areas), or firm program rules (e.g. no youth may be alone in another youth's room) are beyond the control of the youth and should not be discussed at Daily Meeting.

In addition to Preteaching, staff members can use spontaneous teaching to teach Daily Meeting behavior. After teaching and practicing a skill, any occurrence of that skill during Daily Meeting should be heavily reinforced with Effective Praise and positive consequences. For example, when youth use the **SODAS-F** method to solve problems for the first time, staff members should stop everything and reinforce all participants with Effective Praise and positive consequences. In other words, once the youth begin to independently display appropriate Daily Meeting behaviors, they should be rewarded and encouraged to continue those behaviors.

For inappropriate behavior, staff members should use prompts and Teaching Interactions during the meeting. This is very effective for teaching a youth, especially when the Teaching Interaction includes a positive correction statement (e.g. "If you can continue this discussion without any more interrupting, you can earn back half the consequence."). If prompts and Teaching Interactions don't work and a youth's behavior continues to escalate, a staff member should stop the meeting and deal with the problem behavior. The meeting can be continued later.

Limits of authority

Even though many topics can be discussed at Daily Meeting, and many decisions can be made by staff members and the youth together, there are limits to the youth's authority. These limits include the following areas:

1. Matters beyond youth control — As stated earlier, laws (e.g. drug use), program components (e.g. consequences), program rules, safety issues (e.g. no smoking in bed), and the like are beyond the control of the youth. Attempts by the youth or other group participants to change such laws or rules would be fruitless.

2. Youth ability — Other issues are within the control of the   Group Meeting participants, but the staff may restrict or enlarge the range of topics open for debate and decision-making, depending upon the skills of the group. A group of youth who are skilled at solving problems and using good judgment would have greater latitude and range in decision-making topics. For example, if the group

was planning an activity and the youth wanted to suspend the Motivation Systems during that time, the staff might agree, if the youth have handled problems well in the past. For a less-skilled group, the staff may deny the group request and, instead, decide on an individual basis which youth should remain on the Motivation Systems.

3. Veto power — Occasionally, the staff and the youth disagree on the magnitude of a consequence for a certain behavior. If the youth decide to change a consequence, the staff can overrule the decision or ask the youth to "take responsibility." That is, the staff agrees to the consequence established by the youth, but if the behavior occurs in the future, all youth receive the same consequence, as determined by the staff. This is used primarily when staff members suspect a conspiracy among the youth or some collaboration for personal favors.

When establishing consequence ranges for new program rules, staff members should remind the youth that if consequences in that range do not work, the staff can give bigger consequences (outside the range), if needed. This is called a "future consequence," because the youth are agreeing to a bigger consequence if the inappropriate behavior continues.

4. Review dates — A review date is set up for all new rules or decisions that are made. Good rules and decisions can be praised while ineffective decisions can be discussed again. Thus, even poor decisions that slip through or are acted on against the staff's better judgment do not remain in effect for long since they can be modified and improved on the review date.

Child-care staff behavior

Staff members are busy during a Daily Meeting. Before a meeting, they decide which staff member will lead it. That person then acts as the discussion leader while the others participate in the discussions and monitor the behavior of the youth.

Keeping in mind the Daily Meeting skills and the youth's individual treatment goals, staff members use Effective Praise to reinforce appropriate behavior during the meeting. They should not overuse praise, but should apply it to reinforce giving input and making suggestions, using good rationales, staying on task, and the first use of newly taught behaviors.

Staff members also use prompts and cues to remind the youth about appropriate Daily Meeting behavior while not interrupting the flow of the discussion. Furthermore, during the discussions, staff members teach the concepts of pleasantness, effectiveness, fairness, and concern by using those words with the specific behaviors that relate to those concepts. By pairing the concepts with the behaviors, the youth can learn the meaning of the concepts and how they can be used in everyday life.

Finally, staff members guide the discussion and keep it focused on the topics, prompt the use of rationales, and offer summaries to make all options clear before votes are taken. (See the following section for more details.)

In the final analysis, staff members are responsible for all decisions made in the program. If the youth decide on consequences or rules that are unfair or abusive, the staff must redirect the decision or veto it to assure fair treatment for all.

Daily Meeting procedures

When a youth has an issue to bring up at Daily Meeting, he or she is asked to fill out a Daily Meeting card (Figure 1). The back of the card is labeled "Pre-Family Meeting." The youth and a staff member fill out this side prior to the meeting to ensure that the topic is clear and that the youth's rationales have been thought through before the meeting. The front of the card is labeled "Family Meeting Presentation" and is completed during the meeting after the discussion on that topic is completed.

During a Daily Meeting discussion, staff members should generally follow the steps on the "Daily Meeting Components" list. Note that the relationship between the agenda and the **SODAS-F** components is shown in the left-hand column. The **SODAS-F** components are repeated for each topic discussed during a meeting. But staff members should not feel restricted by this proposed agenda. The main focus is to make decisions reasonably and efficiently, and that goal might be best served sometimes by allowing the discussion to take a different course. Again, staff members are encouraged to use their good judgment to arrive at what is best for the youth during any Daily Meeting.

Figure 1

Front

Family Meeting Presentation

\# of youth present: _____   Date: _____

Preparation by: _____

Decision reached: _____

_____

_____

_____

☐ F.T.   ☐ Peers   ☐ Both/   ☐ Youths accepted responsibility

☐ Consensus

☐ Majority   Review Date: _____

# of youth who thought this meeting was:		
☐ Fair	Yes _____	No _____
☐ Pleasant	Yes _____	No _____
☐ Effective	Yes _____	No _____

Back

Pre-Family Meeting

Date: _____

1. Topic for discussion: _____

_____

2. Rationales to be given at family meeting:

   (a) _____

   (b) _____

3.   Specifics decided/discussed before meeting

☐	New rule	
☐	Rule change	
☐	Consequence	
☐	Other _____	

4. Responsible signature: _____ (Youth)

                                      _____ (F.T.)

Daily Meeting components

Bring Meeting to Order

S Identify Issue — use Daily Meeting card

O Youth Input

D Rationales — use concepts of fairness,

A pleasantness, and concern

D Discuss Possible Consequences — use concepts of fairness,

A pleasantness, effectiveness, and concern

S Voting

F Discuss Follow-up for Decision Made (use concepts)

Set Review Date

▶ Reporting problems

Staff members must teach the youth that the "group" has each member's best interests at heart. This includes looking out for each person in the program so that problems can be identified and solved. Everyone's goal should be to help one another. "Everyone" does not just include the staff, schoolteachers, and other adults; "everyone" means the youth, too. This means that each youth is expected to report his or her own problems and inappropriate behaviors, and those of his or her peers.

The youth need to learn that reporting problems is a way of showing concern for themselves and for others. It is not tattling. It shows they care enough to point out problems and enlist the help of the staff and other youth in the program to solve the problem. The youth also need to learn that reporting problems is a form of self-discipline and self-guidance. Everyone has a chance to decide on rules at Group Meeting. The rules are something the whole group believes in, not just the child-care staff. Thus, monitoring and complying with the rules, and reporting rule violations when they occur are tasks for the entire group, not just staff members. This kind of self-discipline is a big part of the Self-Government System enjoyed by the youth in Boys Town programs.

Obviously, reporting problems is designed to help the youth stay out of trouble. Staff members cannot be everywhere at once; a good reporting system improves the staff's ability to monitor all the youth's behavior each day. The youth come to appreciate this as they learn that the group shares a common reputation because they all live in the same facility. They come to see that they share responsibility for one another and have a common interest in their collective good behavior.

Because it is so important for youth to learn to take responsibilities for what happens in the treatment facility, the concept should be introduced to a youth very soon after he or she enters a program. To encourage youth to take on this responsibility, staff members need to award positive consequences to youth who show concern in that way. The youth need to understand that if they do not report the inappropriate behaviors of their peers, it not only shows a lack of concern, but also it makes them accomplices to the misbehavior. Thus, if Jim did something and Frank and John saw it but did not report it, Frank and John would end up with a consequence too, but not one as large as Jim's.

There are three levels of consequences based on the reporting system:

1. Self-report — If a youth does something inappropriate and then promptly reports the problem to a staff member, he or she receives a consequence (based on the misdeed), but earns back part of the consequence for making a self-report.

2. Peer report — If a youth does something inappropriate and another youth reports it to a staff member, the first youth receives a larger-than-normal consequence and the youth who reported the incident receives a substantial positive consequence.

3. Public report — If a youth does something inappropriate and someone outside of the "group" (e.g. neighbor, teacher, policeman, parent) reports it to a staff member, the youth receives a larger-than-normal consequence for the misbehavior and an additional consequence for the "public report" of misbehavior. In this case, if other youth knew about the incident and did not report it, they would receive a consequence similar to that given for the "public report."

Thus, self-reports result in the smallest consequences, while public reports always result in a more substantial consequence. If a youth actively discourages a peer from engaging in inappropriate behavior, that youth would earn a positive consequence and praise from the staff for showing his or her concern for others in the program.

Dimensions of a peer report

When a staff member receives a peer report, he or she must carefully weigh several factors before acting on the report.

1. Has the youth who made the report given feedback to the offender youth? Did the youth who witnessed the incident try to intervene to prevent the incident? This is the kind of prosocial peer group the child-care staff wants to develop. If the reporting youth tried to intervene but the offender youth went ahead and did it anyway, the peer report becomes more important.

2. How serious is the behavior being reported? Does the report concern a petty incident (e.g. John didn't turn off the light when he left the bathroom) or a more serious one? Reports of petty incidents amount to tattling, which often can be ignored by the staff. Reports of more serious misbehaviors are more important and staff members should always act on them.

3. Does this youth frequently report on other youth? A youth who does this frequently, especially for minor or petty incidents, might be trying to manipulate the staff or another youth. A "frequent reporter" should be questioned more thoroughly to establish the importance and relevance of the peer report.

4. Is anyone else affected by the report? Reports that concern several youth in the program might be attempts to manipulate a situation to the benefit of the reporting youth. These reports need to be examined closely before any action is taken.

5. Is the youth willing to bring the report to Daily Meeting? Staff members should encourage youth to present their peer reports and self-reports openly at Daily Meetings. In this way, reports can be made and discussed by the group, and outcomes can be decided by the group. If a youth is unwilling to present a

report at Daily Meeting, the staff should use the opportunity to teach the youth how to bring up and discuss the report. If the youth still is unwilling, staff members should t a k e another look at the report itself.

6. Can a youth benefit from the peer report? The goal of peer reporting is to help each youth stay out of trouble and accomplish prosocial treatment goals. Thus, peer reports need to be constructive, not destructive. Peer reports need to focus on helping a youth become a better person, not on punishment.

As these six points demonstrate, all peer reports are not the same. Some are petty, manipulative, or unimportant. Most, however, are reports of more serious behaviors that deserve to be brought up, discussed, and decided on by the group. Staff members must decide which reports fit into which category and act on them accordingly.

▶ Manager System

The Manager System is the third and final component of the Self-Government System within the Boys Town Family Home Program. In the Manager System, one youth is given the responsibility of monitoring and providing consequences for specified behaviors of the other youth in the program. Although the manager has some advanced responsibilities, he or she is not a staff member. Staff members have a broad range of responsibilities and a great deal of decision-making authority. A manager has only a few prespecified duties and limited decisions to make.

The staff might consider it easier not to have a Manager System. It takes a lot of time and effort to establish and maintain one, more than would be required if the staff members simply handled the manager's duties. But the extra effort is necessary because the youth benefit from the system. The Manager System helps to teach leadership qualities and taking responsibility for others, and the specific behaviors that relate to those concepts. Furthermore, the Manager System is another way for the youth to contribute to the program and, therefore, increase their commitment to the program. The youth contribute by electing the manager and evaluating his or her performance each day at the Daily Meeting. Finally, the Manager System provides the youth with a better understanding and appreciation of the child-care staff's job. They get to share in supervision tasks and feel what it is like to try to maintain a cooperative and pleasant social environment.

Characteristics of the Manager System

1. Managers are elected — The manager is elected by a vote of the other youth at Daily Meeting. The term may last from one day to one week.

2. Managers are trained — Staff members use Preventive Teaching to prepare a manager for his or her responsibilities.

3. Managers are evaluated — Each day, the manager's performance is evaluated by the other youth during the Daily Meeting. The manager can earn positive or negative consequences based upon their assessment of his or her performance.

4. Managers can be recalled — A manager can be recalled at any time by the staff or by a vote of the youth at Daily Meeting.

5. Any youth can be manager — Any youth in the program can be manager, regardless of the Motivation System he or she might be on.

Initiating the Manager System

The staff can consider initiating the Manager System when a majority of the youth:

— can accept negative feedback such as corrective criticism and negative consequences without serious problems.

— can exhibit basic instruction-following skills.

— know the basic program routine.

— can discuss consequences for other youth during Daily Meeting.

Accomplishing these four criteria might take two to four weeks.

Introducing the Manager System

The Manager System can be introduced over the course of two or three Daily Meetings, or it may be done individually. Staff members should describe what the Manager System is and why it is important. This gives the youth a chance to discuss the staff members' rationales and add their own reasons as well. The staff then can discuss the advantages of being a manager. For example, the manager

has substantial power and responsibility for others, and that can be a source of pride and self-esteem. Furthermore, the manager has no daily chore (as other youth do) and can earn positive consequences and extra privileges. Finally, the manager receives much praise from the staff and other youth for doing a good job, and receives special recognition from visitors for the special status.

Once the youth understand the Manager System well, the youth and the child-care staff can decide on the duties for the manager. Some possible duties are:

1. Monitor wake up

2. Check bedroom maintenance before school

3. Check clean-up after breakfast

4. Monitor departure for school

5. Check to make sure the lights and radios are off before youth leave for school

6. Check daily chores

7. Check dinner clean-up

8. Monitor bedtime

A new manager might start with one or two duties. The group can vote to add a few more as the manager's skills develop. After the duties are decided, the youth and staff members should decide how much authority the manager will have. For example, the manager might be granted the authority to give positive consequences and negative consequences, and to offer Effective Praise for tasks that are under way and progressing well. However, the manager might be asked to notify a staff member, rather than attempt to teach social skills, if a problem arises.

In this situation, for example, the manager would be responsible for checking bedroom maintenance and giving a limited consequence, but would not be responsible for dealing with a youth who did not follow instructions or accept feedback well. However, the staff would remind the youth at every Daily Meeting that feedback from a manager is the same as feedback from a staff member. The staff can use Preventive Teaching and then Corrective Teaching when a youth fails to accept feedback on following instructions from a manager.

Following these discussions, staff members can appoint a responsible youth as manager to help model appropriate manager behavior, and to help assure a successful beginning for the Manager System. When the staff is satisfied that other youth can handle the manager's responsibilities, youth can vote for a new manager.

Training for managers

To be effective, a manager needs to learn the criteria for judging each maintenance job (these are written out in detail), how to accept feedback from peers when they review the manager's performance during Daily Meeting, and how to give positive and negative feedback. When a manager gives positive feedback, he or she should follow these steps:

1. Offer Praise

2. Describe Appropriate Behavior

3. Provide Positive Consequences

4. Give a Rationale

When giving negative feedback, a manager should follow these steps:

1. Offer Praise

2. Describe Inappropriate Behavior

3. Provide Consequences — Use Positive Correction

4. Describe Appropriate Behavior

5. Give a Rationale

6. Request Acknowledgment

7. Ask Youth to Redo the Task

8. Report to Staff Member

9. Check Task Again

Staff members teach the manager these skills over the course of a few days. First, the manager goes along with staff members and watches them carry out the manager's duties. Then, staff members have practice sessions to teach the youth the specific skills and watch as he or she tries out the new skills with another youth. Based on this observation, staff members provide feedback and further practice, if necessary. Finally, staff members observe the manager carry out the manager's duties and provide more detailed feedback and training as needed.

Evaluating the manager

Each day at Daily Meeting, the manager receives verbal feedback from the other youth and the child-care staff. Based on their collective observations, the staff members award positive consequences for being a good manager. Of course, if the manager has done an especially poor job, the staff also can give negative consequences and the manager can be subject to a recall vote.

The criteria for evaluating a manager include:

1. Did the manager check all required maintenance and maintain criteria for neatness and thoroughness?

2. Was the manager positive, pleasant, and reinforcing?

3. Did the manager give negative feedback in a calm and objective manner?

4. Was the manager fair and did he or she treat everyone equally without showing favoritism?

5. Did the manager accept positive and negative feedback well during the Daily Meeting review of the manager's performance?

With Preventive Teaching, frequent observation, and immediate feedback over the first few days, most youth develop into very good managers. Managers that are "too easy" don't get the job done while managers that are "too hard" get a lot of feedback from their peers. With practice and sensitive feedback, the Manager System becomes a powerful component of the Self-Government System.

▶ Summary

Boys Town's Self-Government System gives each youth an opportunity to participate in decisions that affect their lives.

Family or Daily Meeting is a daily meeting at which youth and the child-care staff discuss issues and make decisions on rules and concerns. Reporting Problems encourages youth to watch out for each other, and is a way for them to show concern for themselves and others. When serious problems are reported, it is not "tattling"; instead, it is a way for youth to tell child-care workers about problems that could have a negative effect on the youth or the facility. The Manager System allows the youth to elect their own supervisor, and helps youth who serve as managers to learn responsibility and supervisory skills.

When youth are allowed to participate in the day-to-day functions of the care facility or home, they feel like they have more control over what happens to them. This can help them become more active participants in the treatment they receive.

▶ Model comparisons

When looking at both the Psychodynamic (Medical) and Cognitive approaches, it is very clear that they do not utilize any form of self-government. Children in these treatment programs typically have little say in their treatment. The therapist makes the treatment decisions, and the child is expected to conform.

It is very unlikely that the Behavioral Model would use any type of self-government, either. Since the child is typically a passive participant in the therapy, he or she is not always aware of the treatment. This would make it virtually impossible for the child to have any input in it. The therapist makes the decisions regarding what and how the child learns.

Self-government is an important component of the Boys Town Model. Boys Town's system allows youth to have some say in the care they receive and in the rules they have to live by. This gives the youth an opportunity to learn how to give appropriate input and also how to define appropriate rules. Boys Town's Self-Government System also allows the youth to experience and learn leadership skills. This can be very helpful to them in other situations as well.

The eclectic-based University of Oklahoma program does not have a self-government component. The program emphasizes the staff's role, without providing a structure that allows the youth to get involved in the program and treatment decisions.

Positive Peer Culture has a form of self-government because the youth are responsible for treatment and the operation of the program. The youth typically can set the rules and make decisions regarding treatment of other youth. Usually, this privilege is earned over time, with youth who have been in the program longer having more input in the structure of the program.

References

Adams, G.R., Openshaw, D.K., Bennion, L., Mills, T., & Noble, S. (1988). Loneliness in late adolescence: A social skills training study. **Journal of Adolescent Research,** 3, 81-96.

Bedlington, M.M., Solnick, J.V., Braukmann, C.J., Kirigin, K.A., & Wolf, M.M. (1979). **The correlation between some parenting behaviors, delinquency, and youth satisfaction in teaching-family group homes.** Symposium paper printed at the Eighty-Seventh Annual Conven-tion of the American Psychological Association, New York City.

Beker, J. (1992). Power corrupts? **Child and Youth Care Forum**, 21(2), 71-73.

Combs, M.L., & Slaby, D.A. (1977). Social skills training with children. In B.B. Lahey & A.E. Kazdin (Eds.), **Advances in clini-** cal child psychology (pp. 161-201). New York: Plenum Press.

Coughlin, D.D., & Shanahan, D. (1991). **Boys Town family home program training manual (3rd Ed.).** Boys Town, NE: Father Flanagan's Boys' Home.

Cruickshank, W.M., Morse, W.C., & Johns, J.S. (1980). **Learning disabilities: The struggle from adolescence toward adulthood.** Syracuse, NY: Syracuse University Press.

Dowd, T., & Tierney, J. (1992). **Teaching social skills to youth: A curriculum for child-care providers.** Boys Town, NE: Boys Town Press.

Eitzen, D.S. (1974). Impact of behavior modification techniques on locus of control of delinquent boys. **Psychological Reports**, 35(3), 1317-1318.

Elder, G.H. Jr., (1963). Parental power legitimation and its effect on adolescent. **Sociometry, 26**, 50-65.

Elder, J.P., Edelstein, B.A., & Narick, M.M. (1979). Adolescent psychiatric patients: Modifying aggressive behavior with social skills training. **Behavior Modification, 3**, 161-178.

Goldstein, A.P., Sprafkin, R.P., Gershaw, N.J., & Klein, P. (1980). The adolescent: Social skills training through structured learning. In G. Cartledge & J.F. Milburn (Eds.), **Teaching social skills to children** (pp. 249-279). New York: Pergamon Press.

Gresham, F.M. (1981). Social skills training with handicapped children: A review. **Review of Educational Research, 51**, 139-176.

Hansen, D.J., St. Lawrence, J.S., & Christoff, K.A. (1988). Conversation skills of inpatient conduct-disordered youths: Social validation of component behaviors and implications for skills training. **Behavior Modification, 12**, 424-444.

Hazel, J.S., Schumaker, J.B., Sherman, J.A., & Sheldon-Wildgen, J.S. (1983). Social skills training with court-adjudicated youths. In C. LeCroy (Ed.), **Social skills training for children and youth** (pp. 117-137). New York: Haworth Press.

Hendrick, C. (1988). Social skills: A basic subject. **Academic Therapy, 23**, 367-373.

Howing, P.T., Wodarski, J.S., Kurtz, P.D., & Gaudin, J.M. (1990). The empirical base for the implementation of social skills training with maltreated children. **Social Work, 35**, 460-467.

Jones, M.B., & Offord, D.R. (1989). Reduction of antisocial behavior in poor children by nonschool skill development. **Journal of Child Psychology and Psychiatry, 30**, 737-750.

Kazdin, A.E. (1985). **Treatment of antisocial behavior in children and adolescents.** Homewood, IL: The Dorsey Press.

Kipnis, D. (1987). Psychology and behavior technology. **American Psychologist, 30**, 393-397.

Klein, A.F. (1975). **The professional child care worker.** New York: Associated Press.

LeCroy, C.W. (1983). Social skills training with adolescents: A review. In C. LeCroy (Ed.), **Social skills training for children and youth** (pp. 117-137). New York: Haworth Press.

Long, S.J., & Sherer, M. (1984). Social skills training with juvenile offenders. **Child and Family Behavior Therapy, 6**, 1-11.

Oden, S. (1980). A child's social isolation: Origins, prevention, intervention. In G. Cartledge & J.F. Milburn (Eds.), **Teaching social skills to children** (pp. 179-202). New York: Pergamon Press.

Patterson, G.R. (1982). **Coercive family process.** Eugene, OR: Castalia.

Peter, V.J. (1986). **What makes Boys Town so special.** Boys Town, NE: Father Flanagan's Boys' Home.

Pikas, A. (1961). Children's attitudes toward rational versus inhibiting parental authority. **Journal of Abnormal and Social Psychology, 62**, 315-321.

Roosa, J.B. (1973). SOCS: **Situations, options, consequences, simulation: A technique for teaching social interactions.** Unpublished paper presented to the American Psychological Association, Montreal.

Spiegler, M. (1983). **Contemporary behavioral therapy.** Palo Alto, CA: Mayfield Publishing Company.

Trieschman, A.E., Whittaker, J.K., Brendtro, L.K., & Wineman, D. (1979). **The other 23 hours: Child care work with emotionally disturbed children in a treatment milieu.** New York: Aldine Publishing Company.

Trower, P., Bryant, B., & Argyle, M. (1978). **Social skills and mental health.** Pittsburgh: University of Pittsburgh Press.

Veneziano, C., & Veneziano, L. (1988). Knowledge of social skills among institutionalized juvenile delinquents. **Criminal Justice and Behavior, 15**, 152-171.

Willner, A.G. (1975). **Teaching youth preferred interaction behaviors to child care personnel.** Paper presented at the First Annual Teaching-Parent Convention, (May), Lawrence, Kansas.

Willner, A.G., Braukmann, C.J., Kirigin, K.A., Fixsen, D.L., Phillips, E.L., & Wolf, M.M. (1975). Training and validation: Youth-preferred social behavior with child care personnel. In G. Braukmann (Chair), **New directions in behavioral group home research.** Symposium at the 83rd Annual Convention of the American Psychological Association, Chicago.

Willner, A.G., Braukmann, C.J., Kirigin, K.A., Fixsen, D.L., Phillips, E.L., & Wolf, M.M. (1977). The training and validation of youth-preferred social behaviors of child-care personnel. **Journal of Applied Behavioral Analysis, 10**, 219-230.

Index